PRISM

編注
前沢浩子
畔柳和代
吉田朋正
Martin Nuttall

KENKYUSHA

Acknowledgements

We are grateful to the following for permission and courtesy to reproduce copyright material.

Curtis Brown for David Lodge's "Thinks..."/ *Discover* magazine for David E. Levy's "Locked in Place" / Penguin Books Ltd for Erich Harth's "Why the Mind Is in the Head" / Time Inc. for Charles Krauthammer's "Of Headless Mice...and Men"(*Time*, March 16, 1998, p.52) / The Johns Hopkins University Press for Stephen Dixon's "The Signing" (from *14 Stories*, pp. 54-59.) / HarperCollins Publishers Inc. for Erich Fromm's "The Art of Loving" (© 1956 by Erich Fromm. Copyright renewed © 1983 by Annis Fromm) / Time Inc. for Nuna Alberts' "The Science of Love"(*Life*, February 1999, p.38-48) / The Random House Group Limited for Desmond Morris' "Gender Signals" (Extract from *Manwatching* by Desmond Morris published by Jonathan Cape) / Time Inc. for Jeffrey Kluger's "The Gay Side of Nature" (*Time*, April 26, 1999)

And special thanks to the following people for their kind assistance and advice: Kazuhiko Sasaki, Philip Tromovitch, Tatsuo Sato, Atsuhiko Hattori, Masaru Wada, Manabu Noda, Yuichiro Takahashi.

まえがき

　若い人たちが本を読まなくなった、というような「ぼやき」をときおり耳にする。確かに、大学の英語の授業で英米の小説をこつこつと時間をかけて読むという風景は、最近ではめずらしいものになった。一方で、テレビ、雑誌、新聞、インターネットなどから、大量の情報が日々、送り出されていて、政治、経済、科学技術についての断片的な知識は、私たちの身の回りにあふれかえっている。1冊の小説や1編のエッセイを時間をかけてじっくり読んでいるのでは、そんな情報の洪水から取り残されてしまうという「焦り」を感じてしまうのかもしれない。けれど、朝刊の記事を切り抜いて読み、テレビニュースを見聞きし、雑誌を読み散らかすだけでは、情報社会の流れにただただ押し流されているような「空しさ」がある。閉ざされた教養主義に浸るのでもなく、新しい情報を慌てておいかけるだけでもない。現在と向き合いながら、外国語を学ぶには、もう少し多様な理由があるはずだ。では何を読み、何を考えようか、特に英語で…。

　私たち4人の英語教師はとりあえず、自分たちが読んでおもしろいと思うものを、ここに集めてみた。テーマごとに各章は分かれていて、それぞれには3つの読み物が収録してある。フィクション、ノンフィクションの区別なく、異なるスタイルの文章が並んでいる。3つの面を持ったガラスに光を当てると、光は屈折し、分散して、7つの色に分かれる。そんなふうに、ひとつのテーマも、切り口を変えてみると、まるで異なった様相を見せるものだ。またいくつかの章では、同じテーマをめぐって、ずいぶん古い時代に書かれたものと新しいものが並んでいる。私たちが日頃、現代社会に特有ととらえている議論が、実は昔から人間が抱えていた課題だということもある。今日の情報の広がりと、遠い過去と、その両方がつながったとき、目の前の視界は大きく開ける。そのような発見をして、おもしろいと思う、そんな経験をPrismとScopeの2冊で皆さんに味わってもらえれば、と私たちは願っている。英語という一つの外国語を学び、使うことは、それまで慣れ親しんでいた現実に対し、ある種の抵抗感を抱きながら異なった見方をすること、つまり新たなPrism, 新たなScopeを手に入れることではないだろうか。

　この2冊はもともと、東京医科歯科大学教養部の英語教材として編集したものである。大学の教育改革のプロジェクトとして支援して下さった

鈴木章夫学長はじめ関係各位に、改めて御礼申し上げたい。また科学的な知識や用語については、学内の同僚たちから多くの教示を得た。ただ、本書は決して医科系大学や理科系学部専用の教材ではない。科学や歴史や文学がどれほど分かちがたいものなのか、ということを、本書がささやかにでも示せればと念じている。

2001年11月

編注者一同

Contents

Mind   1
- **Thinks . . .** (2001)   by David Lodge — 2
- **Locked in Place** (1998)   by David E. Levy — 12
- **Why the Mind Is in the Head** (1993)   by Erich Harth — 20

Body   29
- **Frankenstein** or the Modern Prometheus (1818) by Mary Shelley — 30
- **Of Headless Mice . . . and Men** The ultimate cloning horror: human organ farms (1998)   by Charles Krauthammer — 37
- **The Signing** (1980)   by Stephen Dixon — 41

Love   47
- **The Art of Loving** (1956)   by Erich Fromm — 48
- **The Science of Love** (1999)   by Nuna Alberts — 53
- **The Nightingale and the Rose** (1888)   by Oscar Wilde — 60

Sexuality   69
- **Gender Signals** (1977)   by Desmond Morris — 70
- **The Gay Side of Nature** (1999)   by Jeffrey Kluger — 77
- **Herland** (1915)   by Charlotte Perkins Gilman — 81

CHAPTER 1
Mind

THINKS...
David Lodge

> **作者紹介**
>   デイヴィッド・ロッジ (1935–) は 1960 年から 1989 年までイギリスのバーミンガム大学で教壇に立ち、文学理論の分野で常に第一線に立つ活動をする一方で、小説家としても現代のイギリスを代表する一人としてよく知られてきた。なかでも *Changing Places* (1975), *Small World* (1984), *Nice Work* (1988) などの大学を舞台とするコミック・ノベルは、学界の今を生きる悲しくも滑稽な学者たちの生態を、軽快かつ知的に描いて、多くの読者を得ている。
>
> **作品紹介**
>   50 歳の誕生日を迎えようとしているラルフ・メッセンジャーは、人工知能や意識の研究の第一人者としてメディアにもてはやされている。グロスター大学の認知科学研究所の所長として迎えられ、富裕なアメリカ女性を妻とし、富と名声をしっかりと握っている彼は自信に満ちており、学界では羨望まじりに「女好き」と噂されている。同じ大学の創作コースの講師として、小説家のヘレン・リードが着任する。伝統的な手法で心のひだを細やかに描く小説家として高い評価を得ているヘレンは、突然夫を亡くしその悲しみからまだ完全に立ち直っていない。メッセンジャーは美しい未亡人ヘレンに興味を持ち、二人はお互いの心のうちを読み切れないまま、惹かれあっていくのだが…。以下はヘレンが初めてメッセンジャーから認知科学なる学問の先端について話を聞く場面。

　On the Wednesday of the second week of the semester, Ralph Messenger and Helen Reed happen to meet in the University's Staff House, at lunchtime. Helen is in the lobby, looking at an exhibition of paintings by a local artist. Ralph [5] sees her as he comes in through the revolving door, and walks up behind her.

　'What d'you think of them?' he says at her shoulder, making her jump.

　'Oh! Hallo . . . I was thinking, if they were *very* cheap, I [10] might buy one to brighten up my living-room.'

'Well, they're bright enough,' he says, surveying the pictures with his head cocked appraisingly. They are landscapes, boldly painted in lurid acrylic colours seldom, if ever, encountered in nature.

'Yes, and they're cheap enough, too. But somehow . . .'

'Somehow they're hideously ugly.'

She laughs. 'I'm afraid you're right.'

'Have you had lunch?'

'I was just on my way to the cafeteria.'

'Why don't we have it together?'

'All right. That would be nice.'

'But not in the cafeteria.'

'I don't usually eat much for lunch,' she says.

'Neither do I, but I like to eat it in comfort,' he says.

The dining room on the second floor is waitress service, and the tables have table-cloths and little vases of plastic flowers on them. They sit by a window with a view of the lake. Helen orders a salad, Ralph the pasta Dish of the Day, and they share a large bottle of sparkling mineral water.

'Actually, I was going to offer you coffee last Sunday morning,' Ralph says. 'I saw you walking in the rain, looking as if you were at a loose end —'

'How did you see me?' She seems startled, and not particularly pleased, by this information.

'From my office window. You walked past the Centre, and I happened to be looking out.'

'What were you doing in your office on a Sunday morning?'

'Oh . . . catching up on work,' he says vaguely. 'I went out of the building to speak to you, but I couldn't find you

---

[29]　**catching up on work**：メッセンジャーは自分の頭に浮かぶことを録音しデータ化して、意識の構造を調べる研究材料に使おうとしている。誰かに聞かれたり、じゃまされたりしないように、日曜日に研究室にきていた。

anywhere. You seemed to disappear into thin air.'

'Did I?' She seems faintly embarrassed.

'Where were you?'

'I went into the chapel.'

[5] 'What for?'

'Why do people usually go into a chapel on a Sunday morning?'

'Are you religious, then?' There is a note of disapproval, or perhaps disappointment, in his voice.

[10] 'I was brought up as a Catholic. I don't believe any more, but —'

'Oh, good.'

'Why do you say that?'

'Well, it's impossible to have a rational conversation about [15] anything important with religious people. I suppose that's why I didn't think of looking for you in the chapel. I had you down as an intelligent rational person. So what were you doing there, if you're not a believer?'

'Well I don't believe literally in the whole caboodle,' she [20] says. 'You know, the Virgin Birth and Transubstantiation and the Infallibility of the Pope and all that. But sometimes I think there must be a kind of truth behind it. Or I hope there is.'

'Why?'

'Because otherwise life is so pointless.'

[25] 'I don't find it so. I find it full of interest and deeply satisfying.'

'Well, you're fortunate. You're healthy and comfortably off and successful in your work —,'

---

[19] **the whole caboodle**：the whole lot
[20] **Virgin Birth**：キリストが処女マリアから生まれたこと。
[20] **Transubstantiation**：カトリックの教義で、正餐式のパンとぶどう酒がキリストの肉と血に変えられること。
[21] **Infallibility of the Pope**：カトリックの教義で、使徒ペテロの後継者であるローマ教皇に絶対的権威を認める考え方。

'Aren't you, then?' he says.

'Well, I suppose so, up to a point. But there are millions who aren't.'

'Let's forget about them for a moment. What about you? Why isn't this life enough? Why do you need religion?'

'I don't need it, exactly. I mean, I've got along without it for most of my adult life, but there are times . . . I lost my husband, you see, about a year ago.'

'Yes, I heard about that.'

She waits for a moment, as if she expects him to add something like *'I'm sorry'*, but he doesn't.

'It was very sudden, totally without warning. An aneurysm in the brain. Our lives seemed to be going so well when it happened. Martin had just been promoted, and my last novel had just won a prize — we were planning to splurge some of it on a holiday. We were actually looking at brochures when . . . ' She stops, evidently upset by the memory. Ralph Messenger waits patiently for her to resume. 'When he collapsed. He went into a coma, and died the next day, in hospital.'

'That was tough for you, but a good way to go for him.'

'How can you say that?' She looks shocked, then angry, angry enough to get up and leave him sitting at the table. 'He was only forty-four. He had years of happy life to look forward to.'

'Who knows? He might have developed some horribly painful degenerative disease next year.'

'And he might not.'

'No, he might not,' Ralph concedes.

'He might have had a long and happy life, and made lots of brilliant radio documentaries and had grandchildren and gone round the world and . . . all kinds of things.'

---

[13] **aneurysm**：動脈瘤
[15] **splurge**：to spend extravagantly or wastefully

'But he doesn't know that now. And he didn't have time to think about it before he died. He died full of hope. That's why I say it was a good way to go.'

[5] The waitress comes up with their food and they suspend the conversation for a few moments as she serves them. It is an opportunity for Helen to calm herself.

'So you think that when we die we just cease to exist?' she says, when the waitress has gone.

'Not in an absolute sense. The atoms of my body are [10] indestructible.'

'But your self, your spirit, your soul . . . ?'

'As far as I'm concerned those are just ways of talking about certain kinds of brain activity. When the brain ceases to function, they necessarily cease too.'

[15] 'And that doesn't fill you with despair?'

'No,' he says cheerfully, twisting creamy ribbons of tagliatelle on his fork. 'Why should it?' He thrusts the steaming pasta into his mouth and munches vigorously.

'Well, it seems pointless to spend years and years [20] acquiring knowledge, accumulating experience, trying to be good, struggling to *make* something of yourself, as the saying goes, if nothing of that self survives death. It's like building a beautiful sandcastle below the tideline.'

'That's the only part of the beach you *can* build a [25] sandcastle,' Ralph says. 'Anyway, I hope to leave a permanent mark on the history of cognitive science before I go. Just as you must hope to do in literature. That's a kind of life after death. The only kind.'

'Well, yes, but the number of authors who go on being [30] really *read* after their death is minuscule. Most of us end up being pulped, literally or metaphorically.' Helen chivvies some

---

[17]　**tagliatelle**：タリアテッレ（幅の広いパスタの一種）
[23]　**tideline**：tidemark

limp lettuce leaves with brownish stalks to the side of her plate and cuts up the remainder. 'What *is* cognitive science, exactly?'

'The systematic study of the mind,' he says. 'It's the last frontier of scientific enquiry.'

'Really?'

'The physicists have pretty well got the cosmos taped. It's only a matter of time before they come up with a unified theory. The discovery of DNA has transformed biology once and for all. Consciousness is the biggest white space on the map of human knowledge. Did you know this is the Decade of the Brain?'

'No. Who said so?'

'Well, I think it was President Bush, as a matter of fact,' says Ralph. 'But he was speaking for the scientific community. All kinds of people have got interested in the subject lately — physicists, biologists, zoologists, neurologists, evolutionary psychologists, mathematicians . . .'

'Which of those are you?' Helen asks.

'I started out as a philosopher. I read Moral Sciences at Cambridge, and did a PhD on the Philosophy of Mind. Then I went to America on a fellowship and got into computers and AI —'

'AI?'

'Artificial Intelligence. Once upon a time nobody was interested in the problem of consciousness except a few philosophers. Now it's the biggest game in town.'

'What's the problem, then?' Helen asks.

Ralph chuckles. 'You don't find anything surprising or puzzling about the fact that you are a conscious being?'

'Not really. About the *content* of my consciousness, yes, of course. Emotions, memories, feelings. They're very problematic. Is that what you mean?'

'Well, they come into it. They're called *qualia* in the literature.'

'Qualia?'

'The specific quality of our subjective experiences of the world — like the smell of coffee, or the taste of pineapple. They're unmistakable, but very difficult to describe. Nobody's figured out how to account for them yet. Nobody's proved that they actually exist.' Perceiving that she is about to protest, he adds, 'Of course they *seem* real enough, but they may just be implementations of something more fundamental and mechanical.'

' "The hardwiring in your brain" ?' she says, putting quote marks round the phrase in her intonation.

Ralph smiles a pleased smile. 'You watched my TV series?'

'Only a little of it, I'm afraid.'

'Well, I don't go the whole way with the neuroscientists. OK, the mind is a machine, but a *virtual* machine. A system of systems.'

'Perhaps it isn't a system at all.'

'Oh, but it is. Everything in the universe is. If you're a scientist you have to start from that assumption.'

'I expect that's why I dropped science at school as soon as they let me.'

'No, you dropped it, I would guess, because it was doled out to you in spoonfuls of distilled boredom . . . Anyway, the problem of consciousness is basically the old mind-body one bequeathed by Descartes. My graduate students call our Centre, "the Mind/Body Shop". We know that the mind

---

[1] **qualia (pl.)**：＜quale 抽象的・普遍的な特質
[28] **Descartes**：(1596-1650)フランスの哲学者・数学者。人間の体を精密な機械としてとらえ、精神と区別して、その二つの相互の関係——「心身問題」(mind-body problem)——を考察した。
[29] **"the Mind/Body Shop"**：せっけんや化粧品を扱うイギリスのチェーン店 "The Body Shop" をもじっている。

doesn't consist of some immaterial spook-stuff, the ghost in the machine. But what *does* it consist of? How *do* you explain the phenomenon of consciousness? Is it just electro-chemical activity in the brain? Neurones firing, neurotransmitters jumping across the synapses? In a sense, yes, that's all there is that we can observe. You can do PET scans and MRI scans nowadays that show different parts of the brain lighting up like a pinball machine, as different emotions and sensations are triggered in the subject. But how is that activity translated into thought? If translated is the word, which it probably isn't. Is there some kind of preverbal medium of consciousness — "mentalese" — which at a certain point, for certain purposes, gets articulated by the particular parts of the brain that specialize in language? These are the kind of questions I'm interested in.'

'And what if they are unanswerable?'

'There are some people in the field who take that view. They're called mysterians.'

'Mysterians. I like the sound of that,' she says. 'I think I'm a mysterian.'

'They believe that consciousness is an irreducible self-evident fact about the world that can't be explained in other

---

[1] **the ghost in the machine**：この言葉はハンガリーの思想家Arthur Koestler が「ホロニクス」という独自のシステム論を展開した代表作、*Ghost in the Machine*(1967)によって一般に流布した。元はイギリスの哲学者Gilbert Ryleが述べた、「心は身体という機械に潜む幽霊のようなものだ」という言葉に由来する。

[4] **firing**：神経細胞の活動が活発になること。

[4] **neurotransmitters**：神経伝達物質

[5] **synapse(s)**：シナプス、神経終末、神経細胞と神経細胞の間の結合部

[6] **PET**：*cf.* p.13 (positron-emission tomography)

[6] **MRI**：磁気共鳴画像。X線を使わず強力な磁気を用いる。

[12] **mentalese**：最近の言語学、特にJerry A. Fodorらの研究によって論じられている内的言語のこと。実際に発話される（あるいは、その可能性のある）いわゆる「言語」のことではなく、言語化される以前の「人間の思考が用いる普遍的なパターン」のようなものを意味する。

terms.'

'Oh, I thought it was more like Keats's "negative capability",' says Helen. She sounds disappointed.

'What's that?'

[5] ' *"When a man is capable of being in uncertainties, mysteries, doubts, without any irritable reaching after fact and reason."* '

'No, these guys are scientists and philosophers, not poets. But they're wrong to give up the search for an explanation.'

[10] 'What's yours, then?'

'I think the mind is like a computer — you use a computer?'

'I've got a laptop. I use it like a glorified typewriter. I have no idea how it does the tricks it does.'

[15] 'OK. Your PC is a linear computer. It performs a lot of tasks one at a time at terrific speed. The brain is more like a parallel computer, in other words it's running lots of programs simultaneously. What we call "attention" is a particular interaction between various parts of the total system. The [20] subsystems and possible connections and combinations between them are so multitudinous and complex that it's very difficult to simulate the whole process — in fact, impossible in the present state of the art. But we're getting there, as British Rail used to say.'

[25] 'You mean, you're trying to design a computer that thinks like a human being?'

'In principle, that's the ultimate objective.'

'And feels like a human being? A computer that has

---

[2] **Keats**：John Keats(1795-1821)。イギリス、ロマン派の詩人。1817年の書簡の中で、シェイクスピアへの強い共感を表明し、不確実、神秘、懐疑に対し、無理やり合理的説明を与えないでおく力——「消極的能力」(negative capability)——が、シェイクスピアにはあると論じた。

[24] **British Rail**：英国鉄道。遅れや運行中止が頻発することで悪名高かった英国の国鉄。サービスの向上を図って1996年に民営化された。

Thinks...

hangovers and falls in love and suffers bereavement?'

'A hangover is a kind of pain, and pain always has been a difficult nut to crack,' says Ralph carefully. 'But I don't see any inherent impossibility in designing and programming a robot that could get into a symbiotic relationship with another robot and would exhibit symptoms of distress if the other robot were put out of commission.'

'You're joking, of course?'

'Not at all.'

'But it's absurd!' Helen exclaims. 'How can robots have feelings? They're just a lot of bits and pieces of metal and wire and plastic.'

'They are at present,' he says. 'But there's no reason why the hardware shouldn't be embodied in some kind of organic material in the future. In the States they've already developed synthetic electro-mechanical muscle tissue for robots. Or we may develop computers that are carbon-based, like biological organisms, instead of silicon-based ones.'

'Your Mind/Body Shop sounds like a modern version of Frankenstein's laboratory.'

'If only,' he says, with a rueful smile. 'We haven't got the resources to build our own robots. Most of our work is theoretical or simulated. It's cheaper — but less exciting. The nearest thing we've got to Frankenstein's laboratory is Max Karinthy's mural.'

'And what is that?'

'I'll show you now, if you're free. And give you a cup of the best machine-made coffee you've ever had.'

'All right,' says Helen. 'Thank you.'

When the waitress brings the bill, Ralph picks it up, but Helen insists on paying her share and he does not make an issue of it.

---

[24] **Max Karinthy's mural**：Max Karinthyという研究者は、メッセンジャーの研究所の壁に、認知科学における様々な理論や実験の絵を描いた。

LOCKED IN PLACE
David E. Levy

> **Introduction**
> 　LIS（ロックトイン・シンドローム）とは、全身が麻痺しているが、意識や知能は機能している状態を指す。「自分という人間の内側に閉じ込められてしまったようなもの」とジャン＝ドミニック・ボービーは著書『潜水服は蝶の夢を見る』で述べている（河野万理子訳、講談社、1998年。原題 *Le Scaphandre et le Papillion*, 1997年刊行）。1995年12月、ファッション雑誌 *ELLE* の編集長だったボービーは脳出血で倒れ、意識が戻ったときはロックインの状態だった。やがて、まばたきを繰り返すことで、彼は本を1冊「書く」ことになる。アルファベットを使用頻度の多い順に読み上げてもらい、使いたい文字が聞こえたら、左まぶたを動かすのだ。
> 　以下はアメリカの一般向け月刊科学雑誌 *Discover*（1980年創刊）に発表された、ロックトイン状態の患者をめぐるレポートである。著者は New York Hospital-Cornell Medical Center の准教授。脳卒中に関する研究もある。

　Each time Andrea stuck her tongue out, it looked more and more as if she was trying to tell me something. I had met her only ten minutes earlier, but I already knew her background. Andrea had sustained serious head injuries in an automobile [5] accident 13 months ago and was not discovered by the police for seven hours. On the way to the hospital, she had had a cardiac arrest. The emergency team was able to restart her heart, but she never regained consciousness.

　Her three grown children had done everything they could [10] to aid their mother's recovery from coma — physical therapy, playing favorite music, stroking her, aromas, and even pleading with her. But after several months without any

---

［7］　**cardiac arrest**：心停止
［10］　**coma**：昏睡
［10］　**physical therapy**：物理療法、理学療法

response, they had grown discouraged and begun seriously to consider how they could help fulfill their mother's wishes. A divorced psychologist, Andrea had discussed with her children the case of Karen Ann Quinlan, the young woman who had sunk into a years-long coma, when it was in the news. She [5] had made her children promise that if she was ever in what was called PVS, a persistent vegetative state, or was severely disabled and unable to express her own wishes, they would permit her feeding tube to be withdrawn so that she could die.

Now, 13 months after entering unconsciousness, Andrea's [10] family, through a lawyer, had asked me to examine her and perform a PET scan on her brain. PET, or positron-emission tomography, is a type of medical imaging done after injection or inhalation of compounds labeled with radioactive isotopes that emit positively charged electrons (positrons). With this [15] technique, we can measure blood flow and glucose or oxygen metabolism in different brain regions.

Investigators at my medical center and I had already studied nine patients in prolonged unconsciousness. Most were vegetative, as we believed Andrea to be. They had [20] sustained diffuse damage throughout the brain from trauma or cardiac arrest. Their PET scans showed striking reductions in brain blood flow and metabolism — more so even than when patients' brains are stilled during deep surgical anesthesia. [25]

---

[4] **Karen Ann Quinlan**：薬物中毒で昏睡状態に陥ったまま10年以上も生き続けたアメリカの女性(1954-85)。生命維持装置を外す許可を求めた養父母の訴えを許可する判決が下され、尊厳死を認める世界最初の判決として注目を集めた。
[7] **vegetative state**：植物状態
[12] **positron-emission tomography**：陽電子放射断層撮影(法)
[14] **radioactive isotope**：放射性アイソトープ
[16] **glucose**：ブドウ糖、グルコース
[17] **metabolism**：代謝
[25] **anesthesia**：麻酔

A few, however, were not truly unconscious but instead were "locked in." These patients usually had extensive damage in a more primitive region at the base of the brain called the brain stem. Within the brain stem is a clump of nerve fibers known as the pons, where messages between the brain and nerves in most muscles are exchanged. The effect of an injury to the pons is a little like the effect that would be produced by severing major telephone communications from a city. The city (the brain) is functioning but cannot communicate with the rest of the world (the body), so for all intents it appears that the city has been deserted. Locked-in patients have lost the ability to control the body voluntarily, but they retain some ability to control the face. Often they can move only their eyes. Although they are conscious, they are unable to communicate. We had studied only a few of these locked-in patients, but their PET scans all showed more normal brain blood flow and metabolism than the PET scans of vegetative patients.

Despite what we can learn about brain function from PET scans, I have always believed that a careful neurological examination can teach us more about an individual patient than such high-tech tools. As a clinical and experimental neurologist, I had examined several hundred patients comatose for at least six hours after a medical catastrophe like a cardiac arrest. Based on simple bedside examinations in the first few days of coma, my colleagues and I developed decision trees — a means of evaluating a set of symptoms and responses — that identified patients whose chance of regaining an independent life was particularly poor or

---

[4]　**brain stem**：脳幹
[5]　**pons**：[解]橋。延髄と中脳のあいだの脳橋。
[24]　**comatose**：昏睡性の、昏睡状態の
[26]　**decision tree**：意思決定のための枝分かれ図

reasonably good. Many patients fell in the middle, where even cautious prediction was not possible. I have never believed these decision trees to be foolproof, but most families (and courts) understand what it means to say that a patient has less than 1 chance in 20 of returning to an independent life. Americans can work with odds, and only a few seem to demand 100 percent certainty.

 The first step had been to introduce myself to Andrea as if she were awake and conscious. In most vegetative patients I see only an impassive mask, but Andrea's face bore a trace of animation. I thought there might be an intelligent being behind it. But this was merely an impression. The observable facts were that she did not speak and she did not move any of her limbs. I asked her to lift first one hand and then the other, and to move her feet. I asked her to look from right to left and noted some eye movement. I showed her several written commands in case she couldn't hear me. No response. I clapped my hands loudly, and her body jerked, indicating that she had not suffered serious hearing damage.

 I then asked her to stick out her tongue. And, slowly, out it came. Once again, and again, out came the tongue. I asked her to do the same when I said her name. Mary — nothing. Carol — nothing. Suzanne — nothing. Andrea — and out came the tongue again. After a few more questions, I was becoming convinced that Andrea's mind was not only conscious but surprisingly intact. I cut to the chase. "What is the square root of 169? Count with your tongue and give me the answer."

 Her tongue moved in and out repeatedly. Finally she reached 13, then nothing more. That was it. The answer. Thirteen. She really was there with me. We established a

---

[26]　**cut to**：（別の場面に）切り替える
[27]　**square root**：平方根

code: once with the tongue for yes, twice for no. It was slow, but I proceeded to ask her several more questions about her life, geography, national history. And each question she got right. By asking questions relating to her care, I soon learned that she could recall several incidents that had taken place in her nursing home room in previous months. She had probably been aware of those speaking at her bedside for at least four months. From staff members, I learned that a few had thought she responded at times to commands. But her responses were rare and inconsistent, and no one was convinced she was conscious. That's the locked-in state — in its way even more cruel than the vegetative state.

Now, the problem. "I understand that you instructed your family to let you die if you were ever vegetative or seriously disabled. Is that true?" Once with the tongue: yes. "Do you still feel that way?" Again, once with the tongue: another yes.

What was I to do? Did that mean she wanted to die? Now? At that point, I thought, I'm the only one who knows she is conscious, and she seems to be telling me she wants to die. I have always supported families in withdrawing care from vegetative patients. I even support patients with terminal illness making such decisions for themselves, as long as they are not making that decision while in the black grip of depression. But I had never been placed in this position. Andrea was conscious; was I not to tell her family?

Andrea's breathing and pulse increased. She appeared agitated. She wanted to communicate something but couldn't. After several false leads of questioning, I realized what Andrea was trying to express. She still wanted to die if she knew she would never improve. But now that her consciousness had been detected, she was convinced that she would receive intensive therapy, would improve, and would actually return to normal. Was that it? Her tongue came out once — yes. I called the family.

It took a little while for her children to accept that Andrea was conscious, but they quickly adjusted. The results of her PET scan showed that blood flow and metabolism in her brain was close to normal — like the few other locked-in patients we had examined and unlike the vegetative ones. Her CT scan, a sophisticated form of X-ray, showed spotty damage throughout her brain, but the damage was worse in the brain stem than in her cerebral hemispheres, the upper regions of the brain that carry out complex mental functions.

Andrea was lucky enough to have considerable financial resources, and that allowed her to undergo extensive therapy. Although it took time and enormous effort on her part, she did improve. Within a few weeks she was able to point with her left hand to letters on an alphabet board and spell out words and sentences. Some time later she got a computer equipped with a program that presented her with a stream of letters; she could press a button to select the letter she needed. After she selected the first letter, the program presented the most likely following letters, and even words, so Andrea's means of expressing herself, while still tedious, became somewhat easier. Eventually she began to speak. Her speech was difficult to comprehend. It took tremendous effort both for her and her listeners, but she succeeded even in making herself understood over the phone.

What was it about Andrea that allowed for such an extraordinary recovery? Unlike most locked-in patients, her brain injury had apparently left important connections intact and allowed her to regain function through sustained effort. That effort, in turn, was fueled by her intense desire to be independent and control her world. Her hunger for independence helped speed her recovery, but it sometimes hindered her improvement. By asserting her need to have

---

［8］ **cerebral hemisphere**：大脑半球

things done her way, she often antagonized those trying to help her. This need to assert control is common in all of us. It is especially understandable when we become sick. If medical staff, families, and others can accept it, tremendous strides
[5] can sometimes be made. But it can also engender resentment and withdrawal in staff, and that happened several times in those working with Andrea.

Sometimes her desire for control hurt her even when surrounded by good will. Andrea was very proud of her ability
[10] to formulate well-structured sentences. The problem was that her speech, though comprehensible, was garbled and thick. Many of us often misunderstood what she said. Despite requests from others to try a different wording, she would repeat the same sentence, word for word, over and over, and of
[15] course we would hear the same mistake over and over. She could have helped communicate but chose instead to dazzle us with her syntax — once (or if) we understood it.

After several more years, Andrea was living, with virtually 24-hour assistance, in her own apartment in Manhattan. My
[20] wife and I met her one evening and accompanied her as she manipulated her motorized wheelchair through the Museum of Modern Art. She insisted on going home alone by bus. On another occasion she and I went to a movie. Afterward, we stopped for coffee. Andrea handled her own coffee cup,
[25] although some of it spilled on her dress. On her fiftieth birthday, she surprised me by taking one or two steps on her own. She eventually persuaded a judge to dissolve the conservatorship that had been established to help her, and she took control of her own finances.

[30] Andrea tried her best to earn money, but her impaired speech made it difficult to resume practice as a psychologist.

---

[28] **conservatorship**：財産管理

Locked in Place

She wrote several articles for lay and professional journals; her training allowed her to present insights that were helpful to many families and patients facing similar hardships. But these articles did not help her financially. She tried to sell her life story as a movie, but that fell through. She served on a local governmental commission for the disabled, but that was a volunteer effort. She was slowly going broke.

The end is consistent with Andrea's life. Eventually her therapy exhausted her financial resources. She saw only two choices: either ending her life or going on government assistance — being institutionalized — and, as she saw it, losing the ability to control her life. She refused to consider moving in with her children or accepting support from relatives. She eventually concluded that her only choice was to commit suicide, and she announced that to the press. Several articles appeared over the next few weeks, and some unsuccessful legal efforts were made to stop her, but she was in full command of her mind. Although she had hoped the publicity might generate contributions, none materialized. She set a private date for her suicide. She knew that her swallowing was so laborious that if she took sedative tablets, she would probably fall asleep before taking enough to kill her. But when she was found dead, the empty bottle of tablets was lying by her side.

She died as she had lived, through tremendous and heroic force of will.

(*Discover* magazine, May 1998)

---

[6] **local governmental commission**：地方自治体の委員会
[7] **go broke**：無一文になる
[11] **institutionalize**：特殊施設に収容する
[21] **sedative tablets**：鎮静剤

WHY THE MIND IS IN THE HEAD
Erich Harth

作者紹介

　エーリック・ハースはウィーンで生まれ、アメリカ合衆国に移住。第２次世界大戦中はアメリカ陸軍の落下傘部隊に所属していた。戦後、ニューヨーク州のシラキュース大学で物理学の博士号を取得した。海軍の研究所、デューク大学、シラキュース大学で長年にわたり脳の研究に従事し、現在はシラキュース大学の名誉教授。著書には *Windows on the Mind* (1982)、*Dawn of a Millennium* (1990) がある。

作品紹介

　心身二元論を唱えたデカルト以来、肉体と精神、つまり脳と心は別々のものと捉えられてきた。今日でも人間の心は脳のメカニズムを超越したところに存在するという考え方が根深く生き続けている一方で、たとえどんなに複雑であっても、脳は解明可能な物理的メカニズムだとする考え方が多数派となっている。筆者ハースは、進化論を受け入れたうえでなお、ホモ・サピエンス（*homo sapiens*＝知性人）は、外部の世界と自己とを分け、創造性と想像力のある精神を持つことによって、他のあらゆる動物とは区別される存在だと主張し、その精神・心の仕組みを物理的なプロセスとして理論上とらえようとする。ハースは、もはや古くなったニュートン的な機械論や唯物論的決定主義ではなく、不確定性や偶然性を基盤とする現代の物理学から精神・心のメカニズムを探ろうとしている。脳と心の関係に新たな見方を提示し、人間の自由意志と科学的な説明を両立させたところに本書 *The Creative Loop: How the Brain Makes a Mind* (1993) の特徴がある。引用個所は、脳が心のありかとして、歴史上どのように捉えられてきたかを説明している。

[5]　When we think hard, we often touch palm to forehead as though to comfort the hardworking organ behind it, and we sometimes shake our heads as if to clear the brain of accumulated wastes and shake it into activity. We take our mind's being there so much for granted that most of us would readily testify that we have a direct sensation of the brain working. But we think we *feel* our thoughts emanating from

our head only because we are told that's where they are bred. The brain, which is the crossroads of all our sensations, in fact has no sensation of itself.

Definitive notions of brain mechanisms, based on the known characteristics of individual neurons, began to take shape in the 1940s. They were inspired by two contemporaneous scientific developments: the rapid advances in computer technology, and a breakthrough in instrumentation that made it possible to observe the activity of single neurons in a functioning brain.

Neurons were found to communicate with each other not unlike the on/off elements in a computer exchanging signals between them. This analogy led to the conceptualization of the brain as a gigantic network of nearly identical and multiply interconnected units; it was called the *neural net*. The staggering complexity of this organ became a powerful argument for "why the mind is in the head." In 1943, in a celebrated paper, the psychiatrist Warren McCulloch, with the help of a mathematician, Walter Pitts, showed that such a neural net could carry out any describable logical function. The authors optimistically state that "both the formal and the final aspects of that activity which we are wont to call *mental* are rigorously deducible from present neurophysiology." They further conclude that "the psychiatrist may take comfort from the obvious conclusion concerning causality — that, for prognosis, history is never necessary." It is important to understand fully all that is implied in the last statement. Everything that affects your brain in the next instant is contained in the *state* of your brain at this instant. Causality is local in space and time. It does not jump over gaps. The present state, if only it were known precisely, tells us everything we want to know about the future.

---

[23] **neurophysiology**：神経生理学
[26] **prognosis**：予知、予測、予後

Mind

* * *

The brain's imperial role within the body has been recognized almost since the beginning of recorded history, with the exception of some notable lapses: the Homeric heroes thought with their diaphragms, and Aristotle, who has misled us on so many things, convinced people for centuries after him that thinking was done by the heart.

We find the brain first mentioned in an ancient Egyptian manuscript known as the Edwin Smith papyrus, whose author is believed to have been a surgeon who lived around 3000 B.C. Among surgical case histories described in the document is a detailed account of a head injury in which the brain was exposed. It appears evident that the author realized the role of the brain as the seat of sensations and bodily control.

Alcmaeon of Croton, rather than Hippocrates, is often called the father of Greek medicine. He lived in the fifth century B.C. and is believed to have been a disciple of Pythagoras. He had performed surgery on the eye, discovered

---

[4] **Homeric heroes**：古代ギリシアの詩人ホメロス(Homer)の叙事詩『オデュッセイア』や『イーリアス』に出てくる神話上の英雄たち。

[5] **diaphragm**：横隔膜

[5] **Aristotle**：アリストテレス(384-322 B.C.)。古代ギリシアの哲学者。「万学の祖」と呼ばれ、多くの分野で後世に大きな影響を与えた。

[9] **Edwin Smith papyrus**：紀元前3000年頃に書かれた外科医術書。紀元前1600年頃の写本が、1862年にアメリカ人のエジプト学者Edwin Smithによって発見された。

[15] **Alcmaeon of Croton**：クロトンのアルクマイオン。ギリシア人の哲学者、医者。紀元前6世紀にイタリア南部のクロトンで、研究目的の人体解剖、生体解剖を初めて行なった人物とされている。

[15] **Hippocrates**：ヒッポクラテス(460 B.C.-？)。古代ギリシアの医学の大成者。病気を身体に起こる自然現象としてとらえ、合理的な説明を与えた点で、医学をそれまでの巫術的な治療法から、独立した学問に成長させたと評価される。また「ヒッポクラテスの誓い」は医師の倫理の礎として現代に受け継がれている。

[18] **Pythagoras**：ピタゴラス(580？-？500B.C.)。ギリシアの哲学者・数学者。クルトンに密儀の学校ピタゴラス教団を創立した。

the optic nerve, and taught that the brain was the central receiving organ of all our senses. Then, almost two centuries after him, Aristotle, in one of his major blunders, announced that thinking is done in the heart, and that the brain served merely to cool the blood and prevent the heart from overheating.

It was Hippocrates who introduced the theory of four *humors*, fluids whose mix determined the mood as well as the physical well-being of a person, thus foreshadowing contemporary brain chemistry. Six centuries later, the Greco-Roman physician Galen elaborated on the humor theory. Brain mechanisms, to Galen, were a matter of hydrodynamics, with the humors streaming through the various cavities, or *ventricles*, of the brain. The idea remained popular throughout the Middle Ages.

But Aristotle's old notion about the heart was far from dead. "Tell me where is fancy bred, or in the heart or in the head?" asks Shakespeare in *The Merchant of Venice*, and Galileo in the beginning of the seventeenth century still finds it necessary to argue that the brain must be the organ of control, since so many more nerves originate and terminate there than at the heart.

---

[8] **humors**：体液。"four humors" とは以下の4体液のこと。black bile（黒胆汁、melancholyとも呼ばれ、憂鬱の原因と考えられた）、blood, phlegm（粘液）、yellow bile（黄胆汁、cholerとも呼ばれ短気の原因と考えられた）。

[11] **Galen**：ガレノス（129‐199/216？）。小アジアのペルガモンで生まれ、ローマで皇帝の侍医を務めるなどして活躍したギリシア人医学者。神経切断の実験をし、神経の支配領域を特定するなど、医学の理論化に力を注いだ。

[12] **hydrodynamics**：水力学、流体力学

[18] ***The Merchant of Venice***：シェイクスピアの喜劇『ヴェニスの商人』（1597）。引用箇所はバッサーニオが箱選びをする際に流れる歌の歌詞。

[19] **Galileo**：ガリレオ・ガリレイ（1564‐1642）。ルネサンス末期のイタリアの自然学者。天文学者。

Still, the brain has never been an organ that elicited much popular attention, especially when compared with that glamor-hogging fist-sized muscle in your chest. There is still the powerful popular notion today that we know things *in our hearts* that the analytic brain simply fails to understand, and the suitor who tells his beloved that he loves her with all his brain is likely to be rejected as a heartless fellow.

The progressively critical, we may call it *scientific*, approach to brain study is shown in the juxtaposition of drawings spanning a period of less than half a century. The first is a famous and much-copied drawing by the monk Gregor Reisch (1467-1525). It is more symbolic than representative, expressing the then current views about brain function, derived to a large extent from Galen. The convolutions of the solid part of the brain merit only a few symbolic swirls that clearly express the artist's view of their insignificance.

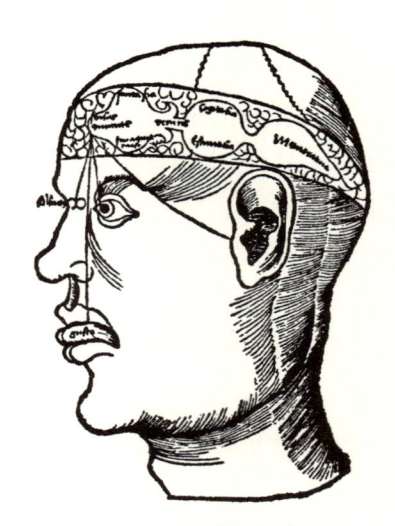

Gregor Reisch

The ventricles dominate the picture. The most forward of these is labeled *sensus communis*. It was believed that the information gathered by all the senses converges there, to be mixed with imagination and fantasy. Our expression *common sense* is derived from that old notion of a single, common sensorium. (In modern neuro-science, this has been replaced by many so-called *sensory association areas*.)

---

[13] **Gregor Reisch**：グレゴール・ライシュ。ドイツの人文主義者で、カトリックの修道会カルトゥジオ会に属していた。
[19] **convolutions**：a sinuous fold in the surface of the brain.［解］脳回
[30] **sensory association areas**：知覚連合野、または感覚連合野

Why the Mind Is in the Head

From the first ventricle the information-laden fluid is filtered, according to Reisch's drawing, through a narrow passage, the *vermis*, and passes to the next cavity, where cognition and thought take place. Another narrow passage leads to the storage area labeled *memorativa*.

Leonardo da Vinci, a contemporary of Reisch, clearly was influenced by the doctrines then current. Unlike his other masterful anatomical drawings, his portrayal of the human brain is like a cartoon. Not even swirls dignify the neural mass he must have seen in his dissections. The cranial vault is empty except for three ventricles that are like bubbles floating in the void.

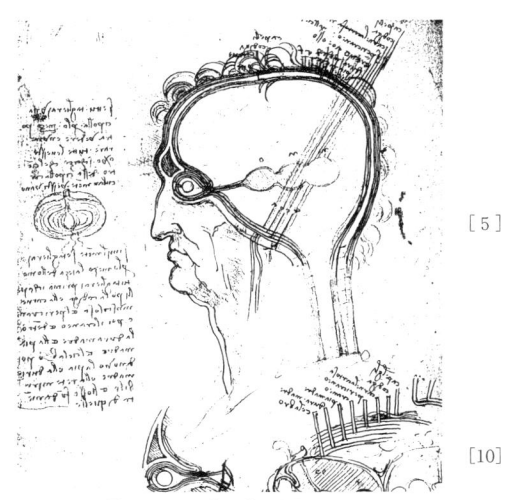

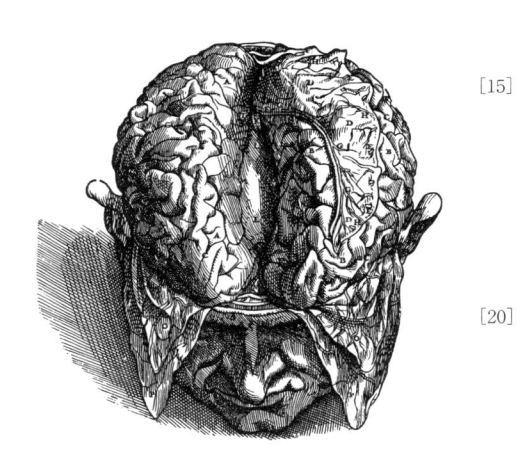

The third drawing is by Belgian anatomist Andreas Vesalius. His monumental

Leonardo da Vinci

Andreas Vesalius

---

[5]　**vermis**：虫様管、虫様水道
[10]　**memorativa**：記憶野
[11]　**Leonardo da Vinci**：レオナルド・ダ・ヴィンチ(1452-1519)。イタリアの画家・彫刻家・建築家・科学者。ミラノやフィレンツェで解剖を行い、その手稿は美術と学問を融合させるルネサンス的精神を反映している。
[21]　**cranial**：頭蓋の
[26]　**Andreas Vesalius**：ベサリウス(1514-64)。ベルギーの解剖学者。ここで言及されている『人体の構造』(略称『ファブリカ』)には、ベネチア派の画家の手になる精密な木版が多く収められている。

treatise *De humani corporis fabrica* appeared in the year 1543, the same year in which Copernicus published his revolutionary book on the motion of the heavenly bodies. Vesalius's work was revolutionary in its own right. In his numerous careful drawings of all aspects of the brain, he does not attempt to express a particular theory of function, but approaches the living form with the unbiased curiosity of a true anatomist. We see here the first portrayal of the brain that looks like a brain.

The notion that fluids coursing through the cerebral ventricles carry out the complex functions of perception, association, memory, recall, and thought finally was replaced by the realization that the brain's activities took place not in the fluid-filled cavities but in the convoluted, solid matter that both Reisch and Leonardo overlooked. Not until near the end of the nineteenth century did scientists realize that the brain consists of highly specialized cells, the *neurons*, whose fibers with their prolific branches link with one another and form a network so vast and so dense that it seems all but hopeless to try to unravel it. According to current estimates, about 200 billion such cells exist in the human head, in addition to a trillion or so other cell types.

What, then, is the function of the ventricles that are embedded in this neural mass? The cerebrospinal fluid they contain is not the carrier of memories and thoughts. For a while it was believed to be nothing more than a kind of cerebral sewer system, carrying away waste products. We now know that it also brings in nutrients and may be the carrier of chemical messengers.

---

[2] **Copernicus**：コペルニクス (1473-1543)。ポーランドの天文学者。地動説の提唱者。
[10] **cerebral**：大脳の、脳の
[24] **cerebrospinal fluid**：髄液、脳脊髄液

Again, old theories don't go away easily. The fluid theory lives on in modern Freudian psychiatry, which tells us that unwanted memories that are suppressed will cause dangerous pressures to build up in the psyche, and must — like an incompressible fluid that is pushed back — pop up somewhere else. This image, although based on totally false premises, has such powerful intuitive appeal that it is considered virtually self-evident. One gathers from it, through seemingly irrefutable logic, that painful experiences must never be allowed to subside on their own, let alone be pushed into the background, but must be *vented* — talked about, rehashed — after which they will rise in the air above the psychiatrist's couch like a flock of departing blackbirds. Opponents have derisively called Freudian theory *psychohydraulics* and pointed out that it is a throwback to Galen.

---

[4] **psyche**：精神
[14] **hydraulics**：水力学

CHAPTER 2
Body

FRANKENSTEIN or the Modern Prometheus*
Mary Shelley

作者紹介

　メアリ・シェリー（1797-1851）はイギリスの作家。母親は思想家メアリ・ウルストンクラフト（Mary Wollstonecraft, 1759-97）、父親は思想家・作家ウィリアム・ゴドウィン（William Godwin, 1756-1836）。16歳のとき、詩人パーシー・ビッシ・シェリー（Percy Bysshe Shelley, 1792-1822）と駆け落ちする。1815年夏、スイスで*Frankenstein*の着想を得て、執筆をはじめる。同年冬、シェリーの妻ハリエットが自殺し、２人は正式に結婚する。1817年５月、*Frankenstein*完成。数社の拒絶にあったのち、1818年に出版される。当初、作者の名はふせられていた。

作品紹介

　探検家ウォルトンと彼の率いる船員たちは北極をめざし航海中、凍えて衰弱している男を助ける。男の知性を感じさせる穏やかな口ぶりと思い悩んでいる様子に、ウォルトンは惹かれる。ある日、「北極について知ることができるなら、命も惜しくない」とウォルトンが言うと、男はうめき、自分の経験から学んでほしいと言う。かくして科学者フランケンシュタインはウォルトンに、怪物を創造した経緯を打ちあける。科学に関心を抱き、生命の始まりに思いをめぐらせ、生について知るために死体が腐敗するさまを観察し、ついに秘密を解きあかして死体に生命を吹き込むまでの日々。その怪物がフランケンシュタインの弟や妻などを殺すに至った過程。こうした話をウォルトンが記録し、イギリスに住む姉へ送る。以下は、怪物がフランケンシュタインに孤独を訴え、異性の仲間を作ってくれと要求する場面。

　テキストは1818年版より。（1831年版もある）

* **Prometheus**：［ギリシア神話］　プロメテウス。水と土から人間を作り、ゼウスに隠れて神々の火を人間に与えた。怒ったゼウスの命令で山に釘付けにされて縛られ、鷲に毎日肝臓を食べられた。プロメテウスは不死で、夜のあいだに肝臓が再生するため、彼の苦しみは幾年も続いたが、やがてヘラクレスによって解き放たれた。

The being finished speaking, and fixed his looks upon me in expectation of a reply. But I was bewildered, perplexed, and unable to arrange my ideas sufficiently to understand the full extent of his proposition. He continued—

"You must create a female for me, with whom I can live in the interchange of those sympathies necessary for my being. This you alone can do; and I demand it of you as a right which you must not refuse."

The latter part of his tale had kindled anew in me the anger that had died away while he narrated his peaceful life among the cottagers, and, as he said this, I could no longer suppress the rage that burned within me.

"I do refuse it," I replied; "and no torture shall ever extort a consent from me. You may render me the most miserable of men, but you shall never make me base in my own eyes. Shall I create another like yourself, whose joint wickedness might desolate the world. Begone! I have answered you; you may torture me, but I will never consent."

"You are in the wrong," replied the fiend; "and, instead of threatening, I am content to reason with you. I am malicious because I am miserable; am I not shunned and hated by all mankind? You, my creator, would tear me to pieces, and triumph; remember that, and tell me why I should pity man more than he pities me? You would not call it murder, if you could precipitate me into one of those ice-rifts, and destroy my frame, the work of your own hands. Shall I respect man, when

---

[9] **The latter part of his tale**：フランケンシュタインの弟を殺し、その罪を一家の知人にかぶせたという告白。

[10] **his peaceful life among the cottagers**：貧しい一家のそばで過ごした日々を指す。彼はこの一家を秘かに観察して言葉を学び、家庭に憧れ、人との交流を夢見た。

[17] **Begone!**：Go away!

[26] **frame**：human or animal body

he contemns me? Let him live with me in the interchange of kindness, and, instead of injury, I would bestow every benefit upon him with tears of gratitude at his acceptance. But that cannot be; the human senses are insurmountable barriers to [5] our union. Yet mine shall not be the submission of abject slavery. I will revenge my injuries: if I cannot inspire love, I will cause fear; and chiefly towards you my arch-enemy, because my creator, do I swear inextinguishable hatred. Have a care: I will work at your destruction, nor finish until I [10] desolate your heart, so that you curse the hour of your birth."

A fiendish rage animated him as he said this; his face was wrinkled into contortions too horrible for human eyes to behold; but presently he calmed himself, and proceeded—

"I intended to reason. This passion is detrimental to me; [15] for you do not reflect that you are the cause of its excess. If any being felt emotions of benevolence towards me, I should return them an hundred and an hundred fold; for that one creature's sake, I would make peace with the whole kind! But I now indulge in dreams of bliss that cannot be realized. What [20] I ask of you is reasonable and moderate; I demand a creature of another sex, but as hideous as myself: the gratification is small, but it is all that I can receive, and it shall content me. It is true, we shall be monsters, cut off from all the world; but on that account we shall be more attached to one another. [25] Our lives will not be happy, but they will be harmless, and free from the misery I now feel. Oh! my creator, make me happy; let me feel gratitude towards you for one benefit! Let me see that I excite the sympathy of some existing thing; do not deny me my request!"

[30] I was moved. I shuddered when I thought of the possible

---

[1] **contemn** : to despise
[7] **arch-enemy** : "arch" = chief, notable, extreme
[14] **detrimental** : harmful

consequences of my consent; but I felt that there was some justice in his argument. His tale, and the feelings he now expressed, proved him to be a creature of fine sensations; and did I not, as his maker, owe him all the portion of happiness that it was in my power to bestow? He saw my change of feeling, and continued—

"If you consent, neither you nor any other human being shall ever see us again: I will go to the vast wilds of South America. My food is not that of man; I do not destroy the lamb and the kid, to glut my appetite; acorns and berries afford me sufficient nourishment. My companion will be of the same nature as myself, and will be content with the same fare. We shall make our bed of dried leaves; the sun will shine on us as on man and will ripen our food. The picture I present to you is peaceful and human, and you must feel that you could deny it only in the wantonness of power and cruelty. Pitiless as you have been towards me, I now see compassion in your eyes; let me seize the favourable moment and persuade you to promise what I so ardently desire."

"You propose," replied I, "to fly from the habitations of man, to dwell in those wilds where the beasts of the field will be your only companions. How can you, who long for the love and sympathy of man, persevere in this exile? You will return, and again seek their kindness, and you will meet with their detestation; your evil passions will be renewed, and you will then have a companion to aid you in the task of destruction. This may not be; cease to argue the point, for I cannot consent."

"How inconstant are your feelings! but a moment ago you were moved by my representations, and why do you again harden yourself to my complaints? I swear to you, by the

---

[10]　**glut**：overeat, satisfy to the fill
[13]　**fare**：food

earth which I inhabit, and by you that made me, that, with the companion you bestow, I will quit the neighborhood of man, and dwell, as it may chance, in the most savage of places. My evil passions will have fled, for I shall meet with sympathy; my life will flow quietly away, and in my dying moments, I shall not curse my maker."

His words had a strange effect upon me. I compassionated him, and sometimes felt a wish to console him; but when I looked upon him, when I saw the filthy mass that moved and talked, my heart sickened, and my feelings were altered to those of horror and hatred. I tried to stifle these sensations; I thought, that as I could not sympathize with him, I had no right to withhold from him the small portion of happiness which was yet in my power to bestow.

"You swear," I said, "to be harmless; but have you not already shewn a degree of malice that should reasonably make me distrust you? May not even this be a feint that will increase your triumph by affording a wider scope for your revenge?"

"How is this? I thought I had moved your compassion, and yet you still refuse to bestow on me the only benefit that can soften my heart, and render me harmless. If I have no ties and no affections, hatred and vice must be my portion; the love of another will destroy the cause of my crimes, and I shall become a thing, of whose existence everyone will be ignorant. My vices are the children of a forced solitude that I abhor; and my virtues will necessarily arise when I live in communion with an equal. I shall feel the affections of a sensitive being, and become linked to the chain of existence and events, from which I am now excluded."

I paused some time to reflect on all he had related and the

---

[11] **stifle** : to suppress
[16] **shewn** : shown

various arguments which he had employed. I thought of the promise of virtues which he had displayed on the opening of his existence, and the subsequent blight of all kindly feeling by the loathing and scorn which his protectors had manifested towards him. His power and threats were not omitted in my calculations: a creature who could exist in the ice caves of the glaciers, and hide himself from pursuit among the ridges of inaccessible precipices, was a being possessing faculties it would be vain to cope with. After a long pause of reflection, I concluded, that the justice due both to him and my fellow-creatures demanded of me that I should comply with his request. Turning to him, therefore, I said —

"I consent to your demand, on your solemn oath to quit Europe for ever, and every other place in the neighbourhood of man, as soon as I shall deliver into your hands a female who will accompany you in your exile."

"I swear," he cried, "by the sun, and by the blue sky of heaven, and by the fire of love that burns my heart, that if you grant my prayer, while they exist you shall never behold me again. Depart to your home, and commence your labours; I shall watch their progress with unutterable anxiety; and fear not but that when you are ready I shall appear."

Saying this, he suddenly quitted me, fearful, perhaps, of any change in my sentiments. I saw him descend the mountain with greater speed than the flight of an eagle, and quickly lost him among the undulations of the sea of ice.

His tale had occupied the whole day; and the sun was upon the verge of the horizon when he departed. I knew that I ought to hasten my descent towards the valley, as I should soon be encompassed in darkness; but my heart was heavy, and my steps slow. The labour of winding among the little

---

[21] **and fear not but that . . .**：but that はやや古風な否定節（"that . . . not . . ." と同じ)、「案ぜずとも時が来れば私からあらわれる」。

paths of the mountains, and fixing my feet firmly as I advanced, perplexed me, occupied as I was by the emotions which the occurrences of the day had produced. Night was far advanced, when I came to the half-way resting-place, and
[5] seated myself beside the fountain. The stars shone at intervals, as the clouds passed from over them; the dark pines rose before me, and every here and there a broken tree lay on the ground: it was a scene of wonderful solemnity, and stirred strange thoughts within me. I wept bitterly; and, clasping my
[10] hands in agony, I exclaimed, "Oh! stars, and clouds, and winds, ye are all about to mock me: if ye really pity me, crush sensation and memory; let me become as nought; but if not, depart, depart and leave me in darkness."

These were wild and miserable thoughts; but I cannot
[15] describe to you how the eternal twinkling of the stars weighed upon me, and how I listened to every blast of wind, as if it were a dull ugly siroc on its way to consume me.

---

[11]　**ye**：二人称代名詞 thou の複数形
[12]　**nought**：naught, nothing
[17]　**siroc**：強熱風。sirocco (*It.*) より。

OF HEADLESS MICE...AND MEN
The ultimate cloning horror: human organ farms

Charles Krauthammer

> **Introduction**
> 　1932年、小説家オルダス・ハクスリー(Aldous Huxley)は「人工子宮」というSF的アイデアを通じて、体外発生の可能性と、その技術的応用がもたらすかもしれない社会的悪夢を人々に知らしめた(*Brave New World*)。そして現在、体外受精や遺伝子操作が現実味をおびるとともに、作家の反ユートピア的な幻想はふたたび私たちのものとなりつつある。高価な遺伝子治療は、「持つ者」と「持たざる者」の断絶をかつてないほど大きなものにしてしまうのではないか。あるいはまた、生物が生物そのものの発生をコントロールするという「論理エラー」に似た逸脱は、どんな「神の罰」も伴わないものなのか。いずれにせよ、そこにあるのはハクスリーの時代と寸分違わぬヒステリックな怒号と、前世紀の作家が決して抱くことのできなかった、はるかに「現実的」な危機への予感なのだ。
> 　以下はクローン羊ドリー誕生の翌年に書かれた、*TIME*誌の記事である。

Last year Dolly the cloned sheep was received with wonder, titters and some vague apprehension. Several weeks ago the announcement by a Chicago physicist that he is assembling a team to produce the first human clone occasioned yet another wave of Brave New World anxiety. But the scariest news of all [5] — and largely overlooked — comes from two obscure labs, at the University of Texas and at the University of Bath. During the past four years, one group created headless mice; the other, headless tadpoles.

---

[2]　**titters**：silly, half-suppressed little laugh
[5]　**Brave New World anxiety**：Introduction参照。題名はシェイクスピアの『テンペスト』(*The Tempest*)でミランダが言う台詞から取られている。

For sheer Frankenstein wattage, the purposeful creation of these animal monsters has no equal. Take the mice. Researchers found the gene that tells the embryo to produce the head. They deleted it. They did this in a thousand mice embryos, four of which were born. I use the term loosely. Having no way to breathe, the mice died instantly.

Why then create them? The Texas researchers want to learn how genes determine embryo development. But you don't have to be a genius to see the true utility of manufacturing headless creatures; for their organs — fully formed, perfectly useful, ripe for plundering.

Why should you be panicked? Because humans are next. "It would almost certainly be possible to produce human bodies without a forebrain," Princeton biologist Lee Silver told the London *Sunday Times*. "These human bodies without any semblance of consciousness would not be considered persons, and thus it would be perfectly legal to keep them 'alive' as a future source of organs."

"Alive." Never have a pair of quotation marks loomed so ominously. Take the mouse-frog technology, apply it to humans, combine it with cloning, and you are become a god: with a single cell taken from, say, your finger, you produce a headless replica of yourself, a mutant twin, arguably lifeless, that becomes your own personal, precisely tissue-matched organ farm.

There are, of course, technical hurdles along the way. Suppressing the equivalent "head" gene in man. Incubating tiny infant organs to grow into larger ones that adults could use. And creating artificial wombs (as per Aldous Huxley),

---

[5] **embryo**：胚
[14] **forebrain**：前脳
[23] **mutant**：突然変異による
[24] **tissue-matched organ farm**：組織が合致する専用臓器養殖場

given that it might be difficult to recruit sane women to carry headless fetuses to their birth/death.

It won't be long, however, before these technical barriers are breached. The ethical barriers are already cracking. Lewis Wolpert, professor of biology at University College, London, finds producing headless humans "personally distasteful" but, given the shortage of organs, does not think distaste is sufficient reason not to go ahead with something that would save lives. And Professor Silver not only sees "nothing wrong, philosophically or rationally," with producing headless humans for organ harvesting; he wants to convince a skeptical public that it is perfectly O.K.

When prominent scientists are prepared to acquiesce in — or indeed encourage — the deliberate creation of deformed and dying quasi-human life, you know we are facing a bioethical abyss. Human beings are ends, not means. There is no grosser corruption of biotechnology than creating a human mutant and disemboweling it at our pleasure for spare parts.

The prospect of headless human clones should put the whole debate about "normal" cloning in a new light. Normal cloning is less a treatment for infertility than a treatment for vanity. It is a way to produce an exact genetic replica of yourself that will walk the earth years after you're gone.

But there is a problem with a clone. It is not really you. It

---

[2]　**fetus**：胎児
[4]　**breached**：broken
[13]　**acquiesce in**：to accept an arrangement, a conclusion, etc without protest.
[15]　**quasi-**：seemingly; apparently but not really
[16]　**abyss**：hole so deep as to appear bottomless
[18]　**disembowel**：はらわたを抜き出す。"bowel" は「腸」。
[22]　**infertility**：不妊

is but a twin, a perfect John Doe Jr., but still a junior. With its own independent consciousness, it is, alas, just a facsimile of you.

The headless clone solves the facsimile problem. It is a gateway to the ultimate vanity: immortality. If you create a real clone, you cannot transfer your consciousness into it to truly live on. But if you create a headless clone of just your body, you have created a ready source of replacement parts to keep you— your consciousness— going indefinitely.

Which is why one form of cloning will inevitably lead to the other. Cloning is the technology of narcissism, and nothing satisfies narcissism like immortality. Headlessness will be cloning's crowning achievement.

The time to put a stop to this is now. Dolly moved President Clinton to create a commission that recommended a temporary ban on human cloning. But with physicist Richard Seed threatening to clone humans, and with headless animals already here, we are past the time for toothless commissions and meaningless bans.

Clinton banned federal funding of human-cloning research of which there is none anyway. He then proposed a five-year ban on cloning. This is not enough. The U.S. Congress should ban human cloning now. Totally. And regarding one particular form, it should be draconian: the deliberate creation of headless humans must be made a crime, indeed a capital crime. If we flinch in the face of this high-tech barbarity, we'll deserve to live in the hell it heralds.

(*TIME*, March 16, 1998)

---

[1] **John Doe**：ジョン・ドウ。訴訟で当事者の本名不明のときに用いる男性の仮名。女性の場合はJane Doe.

[24] **draconian**：過酷な(紀元前7世紀アテネの執政官ドラコン〔Draco〕が発布した刑法が過酷であったことからくる)

[25] **capital crime**：死罪

THE SIGNING
Stephen Dixon

> **作者紹介**
> スティーヴン・ディクソンは 1936 年生まれ。アメリカの作家。中学教員、スクールバスの運転手、ウェイター、バーテンなどさまざまな仕事をしながら執筆、四十代になってから著作が出版されるようになる。多くの短篇によって知られ、生まれ育ったニューヨークを舞台にした作品が多い。"The Signing" では妻を失い、生活の基盤が揺らいでしまった男を描いている。

My wife dies. Now I'm alone. I kiss her hands and leave the hospital room. A nurse runs after me as I walk down the hall.

"Are you going to make arrangements now for the deceased?" he says. [5]

"No."

"Then what do you want us to do with the body?"

"Burn it."

"That's not our job."

"Give it to science." [10]

"You'll have to sign the proper legal papers."

"Give me them."

"They take a while to draw up. Why don't you wait in the guest lounge?"

"I haven't time." [15]

"And her toilet things and radio and clothes."

"I have to go." I ring for the elevator.

"You can't do that."

"I am."

---

[13] **draw up**：作成する
[19] **"I am."**："I am going."

The elevator comes.

"Doctor, doctor," he yells to a doctor going through some files at the nurses' station. She stands up. "What is it nurse?" she says. The elevator door closes. It opens on several floors before it reaches the lobby. I head for the outside. There's a security guard sitting beside the revolving door. He looks like a regular city policeman other than for his hair, which hangs down past his shoulders, and he also has a beard. Most city policemen don't; maybe all. He gets a call on his portable two-way set as I step into one of the quarters of the revolving door. "Laslo." he says into it. I'm outside. "Hey you," he says. I turn around. He's nodding and pointing to me and waves for me to come back. I cross the avenue to get to the bus stop. He comes outside and slips the two-way into his back pocket and walks up to me as I wait for the bus.

"They want you back upstairs to sign some papers," he says.

"Too late. She's dead. I'm alone. I kissed her hands. You can have the body. I just want to be far away from here and as soon as I can."

"They asked me to bring you back."

"You can't. This is a public street. You need a city policeman to take me back, and even then I don't think he or she would be in their rights."

"I'm going to get one."

The bus comes. Its door opens. I have the required exact fare. I step up and put my change in the coin box.

"Don't take this man," the guard says to the bus driver. "They want him back at the hospital there. Something about his wife who was or is a patient, though I don't know the actual reason they want him for."

---

[9] **two-way set**：無線機

The Signing

"I've done nothing," I tell the driver and take a seat in the rear of the bus. A woman sitting in front of me says, "What's holding him up? This isn't a red light."

"Listen," the driver says to the guard, "If you have no specific charge or warrant against this guy, I think I better go." [5]

"Will you please get this bus rolling again?" a passenger says.

"Yes," I say, disguising my voice so they won't think it's me but some other passenger, "I've an important appointment and your slowpokey driving and intermittent dawdling has already made me ten minutes late." [10]

The driver shrugs at the guard. "In or out, friend, but unless you can come up with some official authority to stop this bus, I got to finish my run." [15]

The guard steps into the bus, pays his fare, and sits beside me as the bus pulls out.

"I'll have to stick with you and check in if you don't mind," he says to me. He pushes a button in his two-way set and says "Laslo here." [20]

"Laslo," a voice says. "Where the hell are you?"

"On a bus."

"What are you doing there? You're not through yet."

"I'm with the man you told me to grab at the door. Well, he got past the door. I tried to stop him outside, but he said I [25] needed a city patrolman for that because it was a public street."

"You could've gotten him on the sidewalk in front."

"This was at the bus stop across the street."

"Then he's right. We don't want a suit." [30]

"That's what I thought. So I tried to convince him to come

---

[5] **warrant**：令状

back. He wouldn't. He said he'd kissed some woman's hands and we can have the body. I don't know what that means but want to get it all in before I get too far away from you and lose radio contact. He got on this bus. The driver was sympathetic to my argument about the bus not leaving, but said it would be illegal his helping to restrain the man and that he also had to complete his run. So I got on the bus and am now sitting beside the man and will get off at the next stop if that's what you want me to do. I just didn't know what was the correct way to carry out my orders in this situation, so I thought I'd stick with him till I found out from you."

"You did the right thing. Let me speak to him now."

Laslo holds the two-way in front of my mouth.

"Hello," I say.

"The papers to donate your wife's body to the hospital for research and possible transplants are ready now, sir, so could you return with Officer Laslo?"

"No."

"If you think it'll be too trying an emotional experience to return here, could we meet someplace else where you could sign?"

"Do what you want with her body. There's nothing I ever want to have to do with her again. I'll never speak her name. Never go back to our apartment. Our car I'm going to let rot in the street till it's towed away. This wristwatch. She bought it for me and wore it a few times herself." I throw it out the window.

"Why didn't you just pass it on back here?" the man behind me says.

"These clothes. She bought some of them, mended them all." I take off my jacket, tie, shirt and pants and toss them out

---

[25]　**tow away**：レッカー車が持っていく

the window.

"Lookit," Laslo says, "I'm just a hospital security guard with a pair of handcuffs I'm not going to use on you because we're in a public bus and all you've just gone through, but please calm down."

"This underwear I bought myself yesterday," I say to him. "I needed a new pair. She never touched or saw them, so I don't mind still wearing them. The shoes go, though. She even put on these heels with a shoe-repair kit she bought at the five-and-dime." I take off my shoes and drop them out the window.

The bus has stopped. All the other passengers have left except Laslo. The driver is on the street looking for what I'm sure is a patrolman or police car.

I look at my socks. "I'm not sure about the socks."

"Leave them on," Laslo says. "They look good, and I like brown."

"But did she buy them? I think they were a gift from her two birthdays ago when she gave me a cane picnic basket with a dozen-and-a-half pairs of different-colored socks inside. Yes, this is one of them," and I take them off and throw them out the window. "That's why I tried and still have to get out of this city fast as I can."

"You hear that?" Laslo says into the two-way radio, and the man on the other end says, "I still don't understand."

"You see," I say into it, "we spent too many years here together, my beloved and I — all our adult lives. These streets. That bridge. Those buildings." I spit out the window. "Perhaps even this bus. We took so many rides up and down this line." I try to uproot the seat in front of me but it won't budge. Laslo claps the cuffs on my wrists. "The life," I say

---

[10] **five-and-dime**：" five-and-ten" ともいう。百円ショップのように、硬貨一枚で物が買える安物雑貨店。

and I smash my head through the window.

    An ambulance comes and takes me back to the same hospital. I'm brought to Emergency and put on a cot in the same examining room she was taken to this last time before they moved her to a semiprivate room. A hospital official comes in while the doctors and nurses are tweezing the remaining glass splinters out of my head and stitching me up. "If you're still interested in donating your wife's body," he says. "then we'd like to get the matter out of the way while some of her organs can still be reused by several of the patients upstairs."

    I say, "No, I don't want anyone walking around with my wife's parts where I can bump into him and maybe recognize them any day of the year," but he takes my writing hand and guides it till I've signed.

---

[3]   **cot**：簡易寝台
[6]   **tweeze**：ピンセットで抜く。ピンセットは "tweezers."

CHAPTER 3
Love

The Art of Loving
Erich Fromm

> **作者紹介**
>
> 　著者エーリッヒ・フロム(1900-1980)は、ドイツ生まれの精神分析学者。ナチズムを逃れてアメリカに渡ってからは、*Escape from Freedom* (1941), *The Sane Society* (1955)といった著作によって、広く社会哲学と呼びうるような議論を展開した。彼の書物に他にない美点があるとすれば、多くの「知識人」の本と違って、それが幅広い一般読者を獲得したということに尽きる。日本でも異例と言って良いほどの紹介がなされ、おそらく「人口に膾炙した」という点では、戦後のマックス・ピカート、大学紛争時のサルトル、70年代のマクルーハンに匹敵するかもしれない。
>
> 　だがむろん、こうした事実は、学者が「一般向け」に書いた「軽妙な人生論」(*The Art of Loving*, 1956)が、ただ薄められた真実ばかりで埋められていることを意味するのではない。読んで分かるとおり、事実はまるで逆なのだから。

　Is love an art? Then it requires knowledge and effort. Or is love a pleasant sensation, which to experience is a matter of chance, something one "falls into" if one is lucky? This little book is based on the former premise, while undoubtedly the [5] majority of people today believe in the latter.

　Not that people think that love is not important. They are starved for it; they watch endless numbers of films about happy and unhappy love stories, they listen to hundreds of trashy songs about love — yet hardly anyone thinks that there [10] is anything that needs to be learned about love.

　This peculiar attitude is based on several premises which either singly or combined tend to uphold it. Most people see the problem of love primarily as that of *being loved*, rather than that of *loving*, of one's capacity to love. Hence the [15] problem to them is how to be loved, how to be lovable. In pursuit of this aim they follow several paths. One, which is especially used by men, is to be successful, to be as powerful and rich as the social margin of one's position permits. Another, used especially by women, is to make oneself attractive, by cultivating one's body, dress, etc. Other ways of making oneself attractive, used both by men and women are to develop pleasant manners, interesting conversation, to be helpful, modest, inoffensive. Many of the ways to make oneself lovable are the same as those used to make oneself successful, "to win friends and influence people." As a matter of fact, what most people in our culture mean by being lovable is essentially a mixture between being popular and having sex appeal.

A second premise behind the attitude that there is nothing to be learned about love is the assumption that the problem of love is the problem of an *object*, not the problem of a *faculty*. People think that to *love* is simple, but that to find the right object to love — or to be loved by — is difficult. This attitude has several reasons rooted in the development of modern society. One reason is the great change which occurred in the twentieth century with respect to the choice of a "love object." In the Victorian age, as in many traditional cultures, love was mostly not a spontaneous personal experience which then might lead to marriage. On the contrary, marriage was contracted by convention — either by the respective families, or by a marriage broker; it was concluded on the basis of social considerations, and love was supposed to develop once the marriage had been concluded. In the last few generations the concept of romantic love has become almost universal in the Western world. In the United States, while considerations of a

---

[21] **Victorian age**：ヴィクトリア女王の治世 (1837-1901) に、大英帝国は世界の覇者となった。その経済や社会を支えた中流階級は、宗教や道徳において非常に抑圧された価値観を持ち、特に性に関するタブーが多かった。

conventional nature are not entirely absent, to a vast extent people are in search of "romantic love," of the personal experience of love which then should lead to marriage. This new concept of freedom in love must have greatly enhanced [5] the importance of the *object* as against the importance of the *function*.

Closely related to this factor is another feature characteristic of contemporary culture. Our whole culture is based on the appetite for buying, on the idea of a mutually [10] favorable exchange. Modern man's happiness consists in the thrill of looking at the shop windows, and in buying all that he can afford to buy, either for cash or on installments. He (or she) looks at people in a similar way. For the man an attractive girl — and for the woman an attractive man — are [15] the prizes they are after. "Attractive" usually means a nice package of qualities which are popular and sought after on the personality market. The sense of falling in love develops usually only with regard to such human commodities as are within reach of one's own possibilities for exchange. Two [20] persons thus fall in love when they feel they have found the best object available on the market, considering the limitations of their own exchange values. Often, as in buying real estate, the hidden potentialities which can be developed play a considerable role in this bargain. In a culture in which [25] the marketing orientation prevails, and in which material success is the outstanding value, there is little reason to be surprised that human love relations follow the same pattern of exchange which governs the commodity and the labor market.

The third error leading to the assumption that there is [30] nothing to be learned about love lies in the confusion between the initial experience of *"falling"* in love, and the permanent state of *being* in love. If two people who have been strangers, as all of us are, suddenly let the wall between them break down, and feel close, feel one, this moment of oneness is one of the most exhilarating, most exciting experiences in life. It is all the more wonderful and miraculous for persons who have been shut off, isolated, without love. This miracle of sudden intimacy is often facilitated if it is combined with, or initiated by, sexual attraction and consummation. However, this type of love is by its very nature not lasting. The two persons become well acquainted, their intimacy loses more and more its miraculous character, until their antagonism, their disappointments, their mutual boredom kill whatever is left of initial excitement. Yet, in the beginning they do not know all this: in fact, they take the intensity of the infatuation, this being "crazy" about each other, for proof of the intensity of their love, while it may only prove the degree of their preceding loneliness.

This attitude — that nothing is easier than to love — has continued to be the prevalent idea about love in spite of the overwhelming evidence to the contrary. There is hardly any activity, any enterprise, which is started with such tremendous hopes and expectations, and yet, which fails so regularly, as love. If this were the case with any other activity, people would be eager to know the reasons for the failure, and to learn how one could do better — or they would give up the activity. Since the latter is impossible in the case of love, there seems to be only one adequate way to overcome the failure of love — to examine the reasons for this failure, and to proceed to study the meaning of love.

The first step to take is to become aware that *love is an art*, just as living is an art; if we want to learn how to love we must proceed in the same way we have to proceed if we want to learn any other art, say music, painting, carpentry, or the art of medicine or engineering.

What are the necessary steps in learning any art?

The process of learning an art can be divided conveniently into two parts: one, the mastery of the theory; the other, the mastery of the practice. If I want to learn the art of medicine, I must first know the facts about the human body, and about various diseases. When I have all this theoretical knowledge, I am by no means competent in the art of medicine. I shall become a master in this art only after a great deal of practice, until eventually the results of my theoretical knowledge and the results of my practice are blended into one — my intuition, the essence of the mastery of any art. But, aside from learning the theory and practice, there is a third factor necessary to becoming a master in any art — the mastery of the art must be a matter of ultimate concern; there must be nothing else in the world more important than the art. This holds true for music, for medicine, for carpentry — and for love. And, maybe, here lies the answer to the question of why people in our culture try so rarely to learn this art, in spite of their obvious failures: in spite of the deep-seated craving for love, almost everything else is considered to be more important than love: success, prestige, money, power — almost all our energy is used for the learning of how to achieve these aims, and almost none to learn the art of loving.

---

[16] **deep-seated** : existing far below the surface

THE SCIENCE OF LOVE
Nuna Alberts

> **Introduction**
>
> 　フォト・ジャーナリズムを代表するアメリカの雑誌 *LIFE* は、1999年2月号に10組の有名なカップルの写真を掲載した。それら10組の夫婦はいずれも、病、子供の死、要職の重責など人生の多くの苦難を経験し、長い年月を共有して老いを迎えている。たとえばヨルダンのフセイン国王夫妻。60歳近い国王が王妃を後ろに乗せてさっそうとバイクを走らせている写真がのっている。2度の離婚の後、3人目の妻を飛行機事故で失った国王は、プリンストン大学を卒業し空港設計の仕事をしていたアメリカ女性と出会う。16歳の年齢差と国情の違いを超えて結婚した二人は、ロマンティックなロイヤル・カップルとして有名になったが、複雑な中東の政治状況を背景にクーデターと暗殺が何度も企てられ、そしてリンパ腫に冒されていた国王は、*LIFE* のこの号が出るとまもなく亡くなった。
>
> 　長年、愛情を抱きあいながら生きてきた夫婦の微笑みには、どのような物語がひそんでいるのだろうか。以下は *LIFE* 誌に写真とともに掲載された記事である。愛情もどうやら科学的な分析ができるらしい。

New research in the field of love and attraction shows that romance — long the domain of poets, philosophers and five-hankie movies — may be ruled as much by molecules as it is by emotion. In fact, scientists now believe that the impulse that drives us to mate, marry and remain monogamous is not a result of mere social convention: It is also a complex mix of naturally occurring chemicals and hormones — Cupid's elixirs, if you will — that helps guide us through life's most important decision. That physiological component, say the researchers,

---

[2]　**five-hankie**：sentimental, soppy
[3]　**molecule**：分子
[5]　**monogamous**：being married to only one person at one time
[7]　**Cupid**：the Roman god of love
[7]　**elixir**：an aromatic solution used as a medicine or other remedy

may help explain some of love's mysteries: why opposites attract, why so many seemingly mismatched couples succeed, why we stick together with partners through even the worst of times.

[5] 'When you fall in love or in lust, it isn't merely an emotional event,' says Theresa Crenshaw, the author of *The Alchemy of Love and Lust*. 'Your body's hormones, each with unique contributions, get involved too.'

Free will, of course, can't be discounted. If you like [10] redheads, you like redheads. If you're a sucker for a beautiful voice, the man who croons 'Night and Day' to you has an edge. But doctors have long known that even that most primal of impulses, lust — the feeling that propels the lonely out the door in search of love — has a chemical basis. It is [15] testosterone, the hormone that creates basic sexual desire in men and women.

Researchers are now concentrating on what happens after one walks out the door and into a wide world of romantic opportunity. What physical attributes, outside the obvious, [20] attract? What roles do pheromones play? When do other, more potent brain chemicals, kick in? The last decade's discoveries in neuroscience let researchers predict — even, for the first time, control, albeit in a limited way — what was once thought uncontrollable: love. 'We are at the dawn of a [25] new beginning, where people may soon never have to suffer

---

[10] **sucker**：one that is indiscriminately attracted to something specified
[11] **'Night and Day'**：Cole Porter 作詞作曲のジャズのスタンダード。1934年のミュージカル映画『コンチネンタル』(*The Gay Divorcee*) で Fred Astair が歌い有名になった。
[11] **have an edge**：have an advantage
[15] **testosterone**：テストステロン (精巣から分泌される男性ホルモン)
[20] **pheromone**：フェロモン (動物体内で生産され、対外に分泌されて、同種の他の個体に行動や発生上の特定の反応を起こさせる化学情報物質)
[22] **neuroscience**：神経科学

the pain of love's slings and arrows,' such as rejection, difficulty in bonding and attachment disorders, says James H. Fallon, professor of anatomy and neurobiology at the University of California, Irvine, College of Medicine. In 10 years, maybe less, he says, there could be brain chemical nasal sprays to enhance love between a couple. 'We're very close. And that's not just happy talk . . . we're like giddy kids at the possibilities.'

Indeed, what scientists believe they already know about matters of the heart is remarkable. To illustrate their findings, follow the story of Mike, a fictional Everyman, as he falls in love.

One night, Mike, single, nervously arrives at a party, gets a drink, then scans the room. Science tells us that, unconsciously, he is already noting the size and symmetry of the facial bones of the women around him. He also studies the women's curves, as research shows that men prefer waists to be 60-80 percent the size of hips, an indicator, however crude, of health and fertility. 'Judging beauty has a strong evolutionary component,' says University of Texas at Austin professor of psychology Devendra Singh. 'You're looking at another person and figuring out whether you want your children to carry that person's genes.'

At the party, Mike subconsciously follows these clues and makes eye contact with a woman, Sue. She smiles. His midbrain — the part that controls visual and auditory reflexes — releases the neurotransmitter dopamine, a brain chemical that gives him a rush — and the motivation to initiate conversation. As he nears, Mike's pheromones reach Sue's

---

[3] **neurobiology**：神経生物学
[26] **midbrain**：中脳
[27] **neurotransmitter**：神経伝達物質
[27] **dopamine**：ドーパミン（脳内の神経伝達物質のひとつ）

hypothalamus, eliciting a 'yes, come closer' look. Why this happens isn't clear, but one study at the University of Bern, in Switzerland, suggests that people use smell as a possible cue for distinguishing genetic similarity in a potential partner — a
[5] consideration in preventing possible birth defects.

Mike is now feeling the first flutter of sexual attraction. His hypothalamus — the brain region that triggers the chemicals responsible for emotion — tells his body to send out attraction signals: His pupils dilate; his heart pumps harder
[10] so that his face flushes; he sweats slightly, which gives his skin a warm glow; glands in his scalp release oil to create extra shine. By night's end, he gets her phone number. The next day, memories of Sue direct his brain to secrete increasing levels of dopamine, creating feelings of yearning
[15] that propel him toward the phone. He calls. She sounds excited. The dopamine released in the base of the forebrain prompts the first strong feelings of pleasure that Mike associates with Sue.

When they meet the next night at a restaurant, his
[20] stomach does flip-flops and he starts feeling giddy at the sight of her. He can think of nothing but that face, those eyes, that smile, as his brain pathways become intoxicated with elevated levels of dopamine, norepinephrine (another neurotransmitter) and, particularly, phenylethylamine (PEA). This cocktail of
[25] natural chemicals gives Mike a slight buzz, as if he had taken a very low dose of amphetamines (or a large dose of chocolate, another source of PEA). This contributes to the almost

---

[1] **hypothalamus**：視床下部
[11] **glands**：腺
[20] **flip-flops**：the movement or sound of repeated flapping
[23] **norepinephrine**：ノルエピネフリン（脳内の神経伝達物質のひとつ）
[24] **phenylethylamine**：フェニルエチルアミン（脳内の神経伝達物質のひとつと考える研究者もいる）
[26] **amphetamine**：アンフェタミン（中枢神経興奮剤）

irrational feelings of attraction — we've all felt them — that begin dominating his thoughts at work, while he drives, as he goes to sleep. 'It's a natural high,' says Anthony Walsh, professor of criminology at Boise State University and author of *The Science of Love: Understanding Love and Its Effects on Mind and Body*. 'Your pupils dilate, your heart pumps, you sweat — it's the same reaction you'd have if you were afraid or angry. It's the fight-or-flight mechanism, except you don't want to fight or flee.'

In the weeks that follow, Mike and Sue's relationship deepens. The first night Mike brings Sue home, he dims the lights and plays a little soft music. The chemical oxytocin floods his body. Twenty years ago, oxytocin was considered a female hormone useful only as a trigger for labor contractions and to induce lactation. In the '80s, research found that it is produced in the hypothalamus by both men and women, helping to create feelings of caring and warmth. As Sue's oxytocin also surges, the couple begin forming a bond. Scientists now think that oxytocin actually strengthens the brain's receptors that produce emotions. Oxytocin increases further during touching, cuddling and other stages of sexual intimacy. It may also make it easier to evoke pleasant memories of each other while apart. Mike can think of Sue and experience, in his mind, the way she looks, feels and smells, and that will reinforce his connection to her.

Next comes the wedding. Honeymoon. Now what? Fast-forward 18 months. At this point, Mike and Sue could be at a crossroads. Science tells us that 18 months to three years after the first moment of infatuation, it's not unusual for

---

[12]　**oxytocin**：オキシトシン（脳下垂体後葉から分泌されるホルモン、主として子宮収縮および母乳分泌を促進する）
[14]　**labor contractions**：分娩時の子宮の収縮
[15]　**lactation**：射乳

feelings of neutrality for one's love partner to set in ('Why don't *you* take out the trash?' vs. 'I dream about you all the time'). For many, there could be a chemical explanation. The mix of dopamine, norepinephrine and PEA is so much like a
[5] drug, say scientists, that it takes greater and greater doses to get the same buzz. So after someone has been with one person for a time, his brain stops reacting to the chemicals because it is habituated. 'The brain can't maintain the revved-up status,' says Walsh. 'As happens with any drug, it needs more and
[10] more PEA to make the heart go pitter-patter.'

   Couples with attachments that are shaky for other reasons (money woes, abuse, irreconcilable differences) may part and — because the body's tolerance for PEA soon diminishes — seek someone new with whom to find the thrill of early love.
[15] More likely, however, committed couples will move on to what science suggests is the most rewarding and enduring aspect of love. Though the same addictive rush isn't involved, ongoing physical contact, not just sex, helps produce endorphins, another brain chemical, and continued high doses of oxytocin.
[20] Endorphins calm the mind and kill anxiety. Both chemicals are like natural opiates and help stabilize the couple by inducing what famed obstetrician Michel Odent, of London's Primal Health Research Center, calls 'a druglike dependency.'

   But in the end, will love's mysteries ever unravel in a
[25] laboratory? Some, like Fallon, say yes. Others, perhaps most of us lucky enough to have experienced true love, might believe — and wish — otherwise. Even in this advanced age of science, where we can transplant organs, map the human

---

[8] **revved-up**：＜ rev up: to increase the speed or rate of, enliven, stimulate
[13] **tolerance**：薬物・毒物に対する耐性
[18] **endorphin**：エンドルフィン（内因性のモルヒネのような作用をもつ物質）
[22] **obstetrician**：産科医

genome and clone our own offspring, we still have not come close to understanding what, exactly, ignites our spark of life, our souls, our very being. Maybe, possibly, that will remain true for the farthest reaches of love.

(*LIFE* Magazine, February 1999)

---

［1］ **genome**：ゲノム（精子や卵といった配偶子に含まれる遺伝情報全体）

THE NIGHTINGALE AND THE ROSE
Oscar Wilde

作者紹介

　ヴィクトリア朝を支配していた厳格な市民的倫理から抜け出して、美や芸術を至上のものととらえる、いわゆる「世紀末」の作家の代表がオスカー・ワイルド(1854-1900)である。堕落した生活をおくりながら永遠の若さと美を保ちつづける青年と、彼の代わりに醜く老いていく肖像という設定の小説 The Picture of Dorian Gray(1891), 予言者ヨカナーンの生首に接吻する美女の戯曲 Salomé(1892)は、世紀末耽美主義の色が濃い作品である。市民階級の因襲を嘲笑うかのように、自らも派手な言動で人々の注目を集めつづけたワイルドは、最終的にはその社会常識によって罰せられる。同性愛の罪により投獄され、2年の獄中生活を送った後、フランスに逃れてパリで世を去った。

作品紹介

　世紀末作家ワイルドは美しい童話も書いた。ここに採録した "The Nightingale and the Rose" は童話集 The Happy Prince and Other Tales(1888)の中の一編である。ワイルドは自身の子供たちのためにこれらの物語をつむぎ出した。貧しい人々のために自らの体に埋め込まれた宝石を分け与え、醜い姿になってしまう像の物語 "The Happy Prince" は、日本の子供たちにも親しまれている。だがそこに描かれた愛は、ときに死と結びついている。愛の幻想は死によって完成され、死を超えた永久の愛へと昇華する。一方で、愛の不毛という苦々しい現実がそれと対比されている。

'She said that she would dance with me if I brought her red roses,' cried the young Student, 'but in all my garden there is no red rose.'

[5] 　From her nest in the holm-oak tree the Nightingale heard him, and she looked out through the leaves and wondered.

'No red rose in all my garden!' he cried, and his beautiful eyes filled with tears. 'Ah, on what little things does

---

[4]　**holm-oak**：(植)トキワガシ

The Nightingale and the Rose

happiness depend! I have read all that the wise men have written, and all the secrets of philosophy are mine, yet for want of a red rose is my life made wretched.'

'Here at last is a true lover,' said the Nightingale, 'Night after night have I sung of him though I knew him not: night after night have I told his story to the stars and now I see him. His hair is dark as the hyacinth-blossom, and his lips are red as the rose of his desire, but passion has made his face like pale ivory and sorrow has set her seal upon his brow.'

'The Prince gives a ball tomorrow night,' murmured the young Student, 'and my love will be of the company. If I bring her a red rose she will dance with me till dawn. If I bring her a red rose, I shall hold her in my arms, and she will lean her head upon my shoulder and her hand will be clasped in mine. But there is no red rose in my garden, so I shall sit lonely and she will pass me by. She will have no heed of me, and my heart will break.'

'Here, indeed, is the true lover,' said the Nightingale. 'What I sing of, he suffers: what is joy to me, to him is pain. Surely Love is a wonderful thing. It is more precious than emeralds and dearer than fine opals. Pearls and pomegranates cannot buy it, nor is it set forth in the market-place. It may not be purchased of the merchants, nor can it be weighed out in the balance for gold.'

'The musicians will sit in their gallery,' said the young Student, 'and play upon their stringed instruments, and my love will dance to the sound of the harp and the violin. She will dance so lightly that her feet will not touch the floor, and the courtiers in their gay dresses will throng round her. But

---

[24]　**balance**：天秤、はかり

[25]　**gallery**：建物の内壁にベランダのように張り出した回廊や桟敷席。この例では舞踏会のための楽団席として用いられる。劇場で照明係の場所として使われたり、会議場で傍聴席として使われたりする同様な上階の場所もgalleryと呼ばれる。

with me she will not dance, for I have no red rose to give her'; and he flung himself down on the grass, and buried his face in his hands, and wept.

'Why is he weeping?' asked a little Green Lizard, as he ran past him with his tail in the air.

'Why, indeed?' said a Butterfly, who was fluttering about after a sunbeam.

'Why, indeed?' whispered a Daisy to his neighbour, in a soft, low voice.

'He is weeping for a red rose,' said the Nightingale.

'For a red rose?' they cried; 'how very ridiculous!' and the little Lizard, who was something of a cynic, laughed outright.

But the Nightingale understood the secret of the Student's sorrow, and she sat silent in the oak-tree, and thought about the mystery of Love.

Suddenly she spread her brown wings for flight, and soared into the air. She passed through the grove like a shadow and like a shadow she sailed across the garden.

In the centre of the grass-plot was standing a beautiful Rose-tree, and when she saw it she flew over to it, and lit upon a spray.

'Give me a red rose,' she cried, 'and I will sing you my sweetest song.'

But the Tree shook its head.

'My roses are white,' it answered; 'as white as the foam of the sea, and whiter than the snow on the mountain. But go to my brother who grows round the old sun-dial, and perhaps he will give you what you want.'

So the Nightingale flew over to the Rose-tree that was growing round the old sun-dial.

'Give me a red rose,' she cried, 'and I will sing you my sweetest song.'

But the Tree shook its head.

'My roses are yellow,' it answered; 'as yellow as the hair of

The Nightingale and the Rose

the mermaiden who sits upon an amber throne, and yellower than the daffodil that blooms in the meadow before the mower comes with his scythe. But go to my brother who grows beneath the Student's window, and perhaps he will give you what you want.'

So the Nightingale flew over to the Rose-tree that was growing beneath the Student's window.

'Give me a red rose,' she cried, 'and I will sing you my sweetest song.'

But the Tree shook its head.

'My roses are red,' it answered; 'as red as the feet of the dove, and redder than the great fans of coral that wave and wave in the ocean-cavern. But the winter has chilled my veins, and the frost has nipped my buds, and the storm has broken my branches, and I shall have no roses at all this year.'

'One red rose is all I want,' cried the Nightingale, 'only one red rose! Is there no way by which I can get it?'

'There is a way,' answered the Tree; 'but it is so terrible that I dare not tell it to you.'

'Tell it to me,' said the Nightingale, 'I am not afraid.'

'If you want a red rose,' said the Tree, 'you must build it out of music by moonlight, and stain it with your own heart's-blood. You must sing to me with your breast against a thorn. All night long you must sing to me, and the thorn must pierce your heart, and your life-blood must flow into my veins, and become mine.'

'Death is a great price to pay for a red rose,' cried the Nightingale, 'and Life is very dear to all. It is pleasant to sit in the green wood, and to watch the Sun in his chariot of gold, and the Moon in her chariot of pearl. Sweet is the scent of the hawthorn, and sweet are the bluebells that hide in the valley, and the heather that blows on the hill. Yet Love is better than Life, and what is the heart of a bird compared to the heart of a man?'

So she spread her brown wings for flight, and soared into the air. She swept over the garden like a shadow, and like a shadow she sailed through the grove.

The young Student was still lying on the grass, where she [5] had left him, and the tears were not yet dry in his beautiful eyes.

'Be happy,' cried the Nightingale, 'be happy; you shall have your red rose. I will build it out of music by moonlight, and stain it with my own heart's-blood. All that I ask of you in [10] return is that you will be a true lover, for Love is wiser than Philosophy, though she is wise, and mightier than Power, though he is mighty. Flame-coloured are his wings, and coloured like flame is his body. His lips are sweet as honey, and his breath is like frankincense.'

[15] The Student looked up from the grass, and listened, but he could not understand what the Nightingale was saying to him, for he only knew the things that are written down in books.

But the Oak-tree understood, and felt sad, for he was very fond of the little Nightingale who had built her nest in his [20] branches.

'Sing me one last song,' he whispered; 'I shall feel lonely when you are gone.'

So the Nightingale sang to the Oak-tree, and her voice was like water bubbling from a silver jar.

[25] When she had finished her song, the Student got up, and pulled a note-book and a lead-pencil out of his pocket.

'She has form,' he said to himself, as he walked away through the grove — 'that cannot be denied to her; but has she got feeling? I am afraid not. In fact, she is like most artists; [30] she is all style without any sincerity. She would not sacrifice herself for others. She thinks merely of music, and everybody

---

[14] **frankincense**：乳香(アフリカやアジアの乳香樹からとれる樹脂で、古くから香料として祭式のときなどに香料としてたかれた)

[27] **form**：beauty, comeliness

The Nightingale and the Rose

knows that the arts are selfish. Still, it must be admitted that she has some beautiful notes in her voice. What a pity it is that they do not mean anything, or do any practical good!' And he went into his room, and lay down on his little pallet-bed, and began to think of his love; and, after a time, he fell asleep.

And when the Moon shone in the heavens the Nightingale flew to the Rose-tree, and set her breast against the thorn. All night long she sang, with her breast against the thorn, and the cold crystal Moon leaned down and listened. All night long she sang, and the thorn went deeper and deeper into her breast, and her life-blood ebbed away from her.

She sang first of the birth of love in the heart of a boy and a girl. And on the topmost spray of the Rose-tree there blossomed a marvellous rose, petal following petal, as song followed song. Pale was it, at first, as the mist that hangs over the river — pale as the feet of the morning, and silver as the wings of the dawn. As the shadow of a rose in a mirror of silver, as the shadow of a rose in a waterpool, so was the rose that blossomed on the topmost spray of the Tree.

But the Tree cried to the Nightingale to press closer against the thorn. 'Press closer, little Nightingale,' cried the Tree, 'or the Day will come before the rose is finished.'

So the Nightingale pressed closer against the thorn, and louder and louder grew her song, for she sang of the birth of passion in the soul of a man and a maid.

And a delicate flush of pink came into the leaves of the rose, like the flush in the face of the bridegroom when he kisses the lips of the bride. But the thorn had not yet reached her heart, so the rose's heart remained white, for only a Nightingale's heart's-blood can crimson the heart of a rose.

And the Tree cried to the Nightingale to press closer

---

[4] **pallet** : a straw mattress

against the thorn. 'Press closer, little Nightingale,' cried the Tree, 'or the Day will come before the rose is finished.'

So the Nightingale pressed closer against the thorn, and the thorn touched her heart, and a fierce pang of pain shot through her. Bitter, bitter was the pain, and wilder and wilder grew her song, for she sang of the Love that is perfected by Death, of the Love that dies not in the tomb.

And the marvellous rose became crimson, like the rose of the eastern sky. Crimson was the girdle of petals, and crimson as a ruby was the heart.

But the Nightingale's voice grew fainter, and her little wings began to beat, and a film came over her eyes. Fainter and fainter grew her song, and she felt something choking her in her throat.

Then she gave one last burst of music. The white Moon heard it, and she forgot the dawn, and lingered on in the sky. The red rose heard it, and it trembled all over with ecstasy, and opened its petals to the cold morning air. Echo bore it to her purple cavern in the hills, and woke the sleeping shepherds from their dreams. It floated through the reeds of the river, and they carried its message to the sea.

'Look, look!' cried the Tree, 'the rose is finished now'; but the Nightingale made no answer, for she was lying dead in the long grass, with the thorn in her heart.

And at noon the Student opened his window and looked out.

'Why, what a wonderful piece of luck!' he cried; 'here is a red rose! I have never seen any rose like it in all my life. It is so beautiful that I am sure it has a long Latin name'; and he leaned down and plucked it.

Then he put on his hat, and ran up to the Professor's house with the rose in his hand.

The daughter of the Professor was sitting in the doorway winding blue silk on a reel, and her little dog was lying at her

The Nightingale and the Rose

feet.

'You said that you would dance with me if I brought you a red rose,' cried the Student. 'Here is the reddest rose in all the world. You will wear it tonight next your heart, and as we dance together it will tell you how I love you.' [5]

But the girl frowned.

'I am afraid it will not go with my dress,' she answered; 'and, besides, the Chamberlain's nephew has sent me some real jewels, and everybody knows that jewels cost far more than flowers.' [10]

'Well, upon my word, you are very ungrateful,' said the Student angrily; and he threw the rose into the street, where it fell into the gutter, and a cart-wheel went over it.

'Ungrateful!' said the girl. 'I tell you what, you are very rude; and, after all, who are you? Only a Student. Why, I don't [15] believe you have even got silver buckles to your shoes as the Chamberlain's nephew has'; and she got up from her chair and went into the house.

'What a silly thing Love is!' said the Student as he walked away. 'It is not half as useful as Logic, for it does not prove [20] anything, and it is always telling one of things that are not going to happen, and making one believe things that are not true. In fact, it is quite unpractical, and, as in this age to be practical is everything, I shall go back to Philosophy and study Metaphysics.' [25]

So he returned to his room and pulled out a great dusty book, and began to read.

---

[7]　**go with**：match, be harmonious with
[8]　**Chamberlain**：国王の侍従、宮廷の式部官
[11]　**upon my word**：これは驚いた(驚きやいらだちを表す成句)

ered by enforcing the ruling that forbade them to touch the bodies of others – even of their parents. Separate hammocks and the rules of decency prevented unnecessary bodily contact.

Aboriginal attitudes to the body were thus influenced by the religious ideology of the Jesuits, but a degree of modesty probably existed before contact. According to Jesuit reports, the men were not embarrassed to be seen naked, while the women preferred to cover their genitals. Maroni noted that young women from puberty onwards wore a small apron made from strings of beads or from cloth.

As for the Creoles, Europeans frequently commented – with indignation, envy or prurience – on the behaviour of Creole women. Slave women wore little more than a cloth wrapped around the waist, reaching to the knees. Free women of colour tended to be more covered, at least in public, but the overall impression was of women willing to expose their bodies.

CHAPTER 4
Sexuality

GENDER SIGNALS
Desmond Morris

作者紹介

　デズモンド・モリスは、「大学と縁を切って言いたい放題言う」*動物行動学者、学問を使った「エンタテイナー」と呼ばれている。1928年にイギリスで生まれ、バーミンガム大学を卒業した後、オックスフォード大学で研究生活をおくった。だが、大学に残り学者となることを嫌った彼は、ロンドン動物園に就職し哺乳類のキュレータとなり、テレビの動物番組の制作も手がけ、一般に知られるようになった。動物行動学者モリスの関心と観察の対象は、魚類、鳥類から、哺乳類へ、さらには類人猿、そして人間へと移っていった。お辞儀のような小さなジェスチャーから戦争や宗教に至るまで、人間という動物の営みを、モリスは行動学的アプローチで分析する。*The Naked Ape*（1967），*The Human Zoo*（1969）など彼の著書は広く世界中で読まれている。以下の文章は*Manwatching*（1977）の一章からの抜粋である。

　Gender signals are clues that enable us to identify an individual as either male or female. In addition they may help to emphasize masculinity or femininity in cases where the sex of the individual is already known. At birth the only obvious [5] Gender Signal of the human baby is the shape of its genitals. Penis means boy and vagina means girl, and that is all the layman has to go on. There are other sexual differences, of course, but since these are not available to ordinary observation, they cannot be classed as Gender Signals. To [10] become a Gender Signal, a sexual difference has to be observable.

　Once the newborn baby is clothed it is effectively genderless, and is often referred to as 'it'. Artificial Gender

---

　＊　竹内久美子『そんなバカな…』（文藝春秋，1994）より

[7]　**layman**：a person without professional or specialized knowledge in a particular subject

Signals (blue for a boy, pink for a girl) can be added, and a gender-linked name is given, but as far as the mother is concerned, the baby is a baby and receives the same treatment regardless of its sex. As the child grows this situation rapidly changes. Many of its Gender Signals will have to await the onset of puberty, but there are plenty of others available. Most of these are imposed on the child by the society in which it lives. Boys will be given different clothes, hairstyles, toys, ornaments, pastimes and sports from girls. Although children are functionally pre-sexual, they are given strongly defined sexual roles. Society prepares them for the future and gives them a gender identity long before they need it for reproductive activities.

This trend has the effect of widening the 'gender gap' between the sexes so that when they become adult, boys will be not only reproductively masculine but also socially masculine, and girls will be both reproductively and socially feminine. This exaggeration of the differences between men and women has come under severe attack in recent years and some people today feel that a strong reversal of the trend should be encouraged. They argue that the gender gap belongs to man's ancient past and is no longer relevant in the modern world.

To some extent they are correct and, to appreciate why, we must consider for a moment the long period when our ancestors evolved as primitive hunters. Over a time-span of more than a million years, early man changed from the typical primate mode of feeding to a system that demanded a major division of labour between the sexes. Nearly all primates wander around in mixed bands of males, females and young, moving from one feeding site to another, picking edible fruits, nuts and berries wherever they find them.

[6] **puberty** : the period during which adolescents reach sexual maturity and become capable of reproduction

Sexuality

When our ancient ancestors abandoned this way of life to become hunter-gatherers, their whole social organization had to be changed. Hunting involved intensely athletic episodes and the females of the group, who were nearly always
[5] pregnant or nursing, had to be left behind. This meant that the group had to stop wandering and establish a fixed home base where the males could return after the hunt. The females could carry out the less strenuous food-gathering near this home base, bringing vegetable foods back from the
[10] surrounding district; but because of their heavier breeding burden, they could not become specialized hunters like the males.

As a result of this divided labour system, the male body
[15] became more and more specialized as a running, jumping and throwing machine, while the females became improved breeding machines. Consequently, some Gender Signals stem from the male hunting trend and others arise from female breeding specializations. Because of hunting requirements
[20] male bodies are taller and heavier than female bodies, with bigger bones and more muscle. Thus they are stronger and can carry heavier loads. Males have proportionally longer legs and larger feet and are therefore faster and more sure-footed runners. Males have broader shoulders and longer arms, and
[25] their forearms are longer in relation to their upper arms. This makes them better aimers and weapon-throwers and since they have bigger hands with thicker fingers and stronger thumbs, they are also better weapon graspers. Males have bigger chests housing larger lungs and hearts. Together these
[30] features mean that males can call upon a greater respiratory response, bringing with it greater stamina and quicker recovery from physical exertion and making them better

---

[8] **strenuous**：requiring or using great effort
[30] **respiratory**：呼吸の、呼吸のための

breathers and long-distance chasers. Males also have stronger skulls with heavier bony ridges, and their jaws are thicker and sturdier. This makes them better protected against physical damage.

Turning to the female, there are several important Gender Signals arising from her specialized role as a child-bearer and feeder. Her pelvis is wider and rotated back slightly more than in the male. Her waist is a little more slender and her thighs a little thicker. Her navel is deeper and her belly longer. Her breasts are swollen. These specializations, which aid in the carrying of the foetus, its delivery and its subsequent suckling, alter the outline of the human female in several characteristic ways. Her protruding breasts mean that her chest, although narrower than the male's when seen from the front, is deeper when seen from the side, even at a distance. The female torso also has a distinctive hourglass shape created by the narrow waist and the wide hips that cover the broad pelvis. Because the thighs start wider apart from each other, there is a larger crotch-gap in the female, and an inward slope to the thighs that often leads to an almost knock-kneed appearance.

Because the pelvis is rotated backwards, the female buttocks protrude more than those of the male. They are also fleshier and wider, making them much more conspicuous. When the female walks, and especially when she runs, her childbearing anatomy gives her a special gait. The inward sloping thighs force her to make semicircular rotations of the legs. Her buttocks sway more and her body tends to wiggle in a way that contrasts strikingly with the male gait. In addition, her shorter legs mean that she takes shorter strides

---

[2]　**skull**：頭蓋、頭骨
[7]　**pelvis**：骨盤
[11]　**foetus**：胎児
[21]　**knock-kneed**：X脚の

and her running actions generally are much clumsier than those of the male.

Almost every natural Gender Signal mentioned so far can be discovered in an artificially exaggerated form in one culture or another. The greater height of the male has often been amplified by the wearing of tall headdresses; the broader shoulders of the male have frequently been increased further in width by the wearing of padded jackets or tunics with epaulettes; the narrower waist of the female has often been exaggerated by the wearing of tight corsets; the protruding breasts of the female have been made to protrude still further by the wearing of brassiere cups and padding. Women have also added padded hips and bustles to their larger hip measurements and their already bigger buttocks. Their large, fleshier lips have been exaggerated by the wearing of lipstick. Their small feet have been made to look even smaller by the wearing of tight shoes, or, in the Orient, by ruthless and painful foot-binding. Their smoother skin is made even smoother by powder and cosmetics. The list is a long one.

It becomes even longer when one adds the pure cultural inventions which have little or nothing to do with the basic anatomical differences between the sexes. Invented Gender Signals are so numerous, so diverse, and often so short-lived, that they can change from generation to generation and even from season to season; they can alter as one moves from country to country or even from district to district. Their most interesting feature is that they *are* so common. It is as if every human being feels the constant need to remind companions of his or her gender, despite the fact that there are perfectly adequate natural Gender Signals available to do the job.

A few obvious examples of invented signals are: short hair

---

[9]　**epaulette**：肩を飾るもの、肩章
[13]　**bustle**：腰当て、バッスル（1870年代にスカートの後ろを膨らませるために使用した）

versus long hair; skirts versus trousers; handbags versus pockets; make-up or no make-up and pipes versus cigarettes. These are entirely arbitrary and although, at the time and place they are used, they seem to be basically masculine or feminine, there is nothing that links them inevitably to one sex or the other, beyond local fashion. Head hair is long in both sexes; it is a species signal, distinguishing us from other primates, but that is all. Here there is no difference between the sexes at a biological level, and the only reason short hair has become associated with males is because of long-standing military anti-parasite regulations. Skirts have often been the male attire and trousers the female garment, if one casts one's net widely enough across different cultures and epochs.

Sometimes an apparently arbitrary difference has an underlying biological explanation. An intriguing one is the answer to the age-old question: Why do males button their jackets left over right, while females button them right over left? This behaviour has been going on for centuries and is usually referred to simply as traditional. The true explanation, however, appears to be that males prefer left over right because it

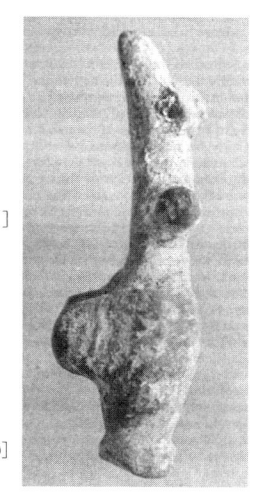

[16]　**parasite**：寄生動物、寄生虫
[24]　**intriguing**：arousing curiosity

means they can tuck their right hands into the fold of the garment. This began in a pocketless epoch and was supposedly a way of keeping the dominant weapon-hand warm and ready for action, and has persisted ever since. Females, by contrast, preferred the wrapping over of the longer right side of their garment because they tended to carry their babies more often on the left breast than the right, and it meant that they could wrap the long fold over the infant as it slept or sucked. Again the pattern is thought to have persisted long after the original reason for it became obsolete.

Artificial, invented Gender Signals may come and go, but those stemming from the human genetic inheritance may prove stubbornly resistant to social progress. Change they no doubt will, but the hard fact is that the process may take another million years of evolution to become a genetic reality. In the meantime, the Gender Gap, though narrowing, will retain much of the fascinating complexity that pervades and influences so profoundly our ordinary everyday lives.

THE GAY SIDE OF NATURE

Jeffrey Kluger

> **ホモセクシュアルは不自然？**
> 　認知科学、言語学の分野で博士論文の準備をしているうちに、Bruce Bagemihl 氏は動物の性行動が予想以上に多様であることに気づく。以後 10 年をかけて調査をし、その結果を著書 *Biological Exuberance: Animal Homosexuality and Natural Diversity*（1999）で発表した。この本は、人間を含む動物にとって「自然」な性行動とは何かという問題に、新たな視点を呈示している。以下の文は *TIME* に掲載されたこの本の紹介である。

Giraffes do it, goats do it, birds and bonobos and dolphins do it. Humans beings — a lot of them anyway — like to do it too, but of all the planet's species, they're the only ones who are oppressed when they try.

What humans share with so many other animals, it now appears, is freewheeling homosexuality. For centuries opponents of gay rights have seen same-gender sex as a uniquely human phenomenon, one of the many ways our famously corruptible species flouts the laws of nature. But nature's morality, it seems, may be remarkably flexible, at least if the new book *Biological Exuberance*, by linguist and cognitive scientist Bruce Bagemihl, is to be believed. According to Bagemihl, the animal kingdom is a more sexually complex place than most people know — one where couplings

---

[1]　**bonobos**：ボノボ。別名ピグミーチンパンジー。アフリカ、ザイール川左岸の熱帯雨林の中に生息。
[7]　**freewheeling**：free of restraints or rules in organization, carefree
[10]　**flout**：to show contempt for; mock; scorn
[13]　**cognitive scientist**：認知科学者。認知科学とは脳と心の働きを情報科学の方法論によって明らかにしようとするもの。

routinely take place not just between male-female pairs but also between male-male and female-female ones. What's more, same-sex partners don't meet merely for brief encounters, but may form long-term bonds, sometimes mating [5] for years or even for life.

Bagemihl's ideas have caused a stir in the higher, human community, especially among scientists who find it simplistic to equate any animal behavior with human behavior. But Bagemihl stands behind the findings, arguing that if [10] homosexuality comes naturally to other creatures, perhaps it's time to quit getting into such a lather over the fact that it comes naturally to humans too. "Animal sexuality is more complex than we imagined," says Bagemihl. "That diversity is part of human heritage."

[15] For a love that long dared not speak its name, animal homosexuality is astonishingly common. Scouring zoological journals and conducting extensive interviews with scientists, Bagemihl found same-sex pairings documented in more than 450 different species. In a world teeming with more than 1 [20] million species, that may not seem like much. Animals, however, can be surprisingly prim about when and under whose prying eye they engage in sexual activity; as few as 2,000 species have thus been observed closely enough to reveal their full range of coupling behavior. Within such a small [25] sampling, 450 represents more than 20%.

That 20% may spend its time lustily or quite tenderly. Among bonobos, a chimplike ape, homosexual pairings account for as much as 50% of all sexual activity. Females especially

---

[11] **lather** : state of agitation

[15] **a love that dared not speak its name** : オスカー・ワイルドと親しかった詩人Lord Alfred Douglas(1870-1945)の作品 'Two Loves' (1896) に出てくる、"I am the Love that dare not speak its name" のもじり。 *cf.* p.60

[19] **teeming with** : being full of

engage in repeated acts of same-sex sex, spending far more than the 12 or so seconds the whole transaction can take when a randy male is involved. Male giraffes practice necking — literally — in a very big way, entwining their long bodies until both partners become sexually aroused. Heterosexual and homosexual dolphin pairs engage in face-to-face sexual encounters that look altogether human. Animals as diverse as elephants and rodents practice same-sex mounting, and macaques raise that affection ante further, often kissing while assuming a coital position. Same-gender sexual activity, says Bagemihl, "encompasses a wide range of forms."

What struck Bagemihl most is those forms that go beyond mere sexual gratification. Humboldt penguins may have homosexual unions that last six years; male greylag geese may stay paired for 15 years — a lifetime commitment when you've got the lifespan of a goose. Bears and some other mammals may bring their young into homosexual unions, raising them with their same-sex partner just as they would with a member of the opposite sex.

But witnessing same-sex activity and understanding it are two different things, and some experts believe observers like Bagemihl are misreading the evidence. In species that lack sophisticated language — which is to say all species but ours — sex serves many nonsexual purposes, including establishing alliances and appeasing enemies, all things animals must do with members of both sexes. "Sexuality helps animals

---

[3] **randy**：lustful; eager for sexual gratification
[3] **necking**：kissing and caressing amorously
[8] **rodent**：齧歯動物（ネズミ・リスなど）
[9] **macaque**：マカークザル（アジア・北アフリカ産の短尾のサル）
[9] **raise that affection ante**：raise the anteは口語で「賭け金を引き上げる」の意。ここでは「前戯で性行動を盛り上げる」というような意味。
[10] **coital**：coital (adj.) ＜ coitus (n.): sexual intercourse
[14] **greylag goose**：ハイイロガン（鳥）

maneuver around each other before making real contact," says Martin Daly, an evolutionary psychologist at McMaster University in Ontario. "Putting all that into a homosexual category seems simplistic."

[5] Even if some animals do engage in homosexual activity purely for pleasure, their behavior still serves as an incomplete model — and an incomplete explanation — for human behavior. "In our society homosexuality means a principal or exclusive orientation," says psychology professor [10] Frans de Waal of the Yerkes Primate Center in Atlanta. "Among animals it's just nonreproductive sexual behavior."

Whether any of this turns out to be good for the gay and lesbian community is unclear. While the new findings seem to support the idea that homosexuality is merely a natural form [15] of sexual expression, Bagemihl believes such political questions may be beside the point. "We shouldn't have to look to the animal world to see what's normal or ethical," he says. Indeed, when it comes to answering those questions, Mother Nature seems to be keeping an open mind.

(*TIME*, April 26, 1999)

---

[1]　**maneuver**：巧みな策で立ち回る、うまく行動する

HERLAND
Charlotte Perkins Gilman

作者紹介
　シャーロット・パーキンズ・ギルマン(1860-1935)は、アメリカの思想家、フェミニスト。みずからを社会学者ととらえ、フェミニストと呼ばれることは好まなかった。にもかかわらず、女性を取り巻く問題をめぐる著作が多いのは、人間社会の「進化」には女性の貢献が不可欠だという信念ゆえである。代表作の "The Yellow Wallpaper"(1892)は、出産後に鬱病に苦しんだ経験を踏まえて書かれた短篇小説。治療の一環として医師から読み書きを禁じられた若い母親が語り手で、狂気を描いた傑作とも、読者に不快感を与えるだけのおぞましい作品とも評された。ギルマンは精力的に執筆し、講演を行なっていたが、晩年不治の病にかかる。人間には安楽死をする権利があると考えていた彼女は自ら死を選び、最後まで問題提起を行なった。

作品紹介
　探険家、医師、社会学者が旅先で「女だけの国がある」という噂を耳にする。好奇心をかきたてられた彼ら三人は、いったんアメリカへ帰るものの、その国を目指して再び旅立つ。そこは予想に反して、美しく、合理的で、治安がよく、本当に男のいない国だった。三人が何より驚くのは、そこに住む女性たちが「女らしく」も「母親らしく」もないことだった。ハーランドの女たちは機敏で、木登りをしたり、駆け回ったり、建物を造ったりする。知性も創造力も持ち合わせていて、生活向上のための研究も怠らなかった。本書の語り手である社会学者は観察をつづけるうち、異国の見事なシステムとそれを作った人々に畏敬の念を抱くようになる。テキストは *Herland*(1915)全12章のうち2章からの抜粋。

登場人物について
　男性は全員アメリカ人。テリー(Terry)はマッチョな探険家。ジェフ(Jeff)は医師、繊細なロマンチスト。語り手のヴァル(Val)は社会学者、科学の力と自分の理性を信じている。女性はすべてハーランドの人。ソメル(Somel)はヴァルの先生。ハーランドの言語や文化を説明し、質問にじっくりつきあってくれる。エラドー(Ellador)とセリス(Celis)とアリマ(Alima)は、森で仕事中に男たちと出会い、友情を深める。やがて三組の恋人たちが生まれ、そろって結婚式を挙げる。"Expelled" からの引用は、結婚後の話。

"The Girls of Herland"

I was good friends with all three of them but best of all with Ellador, long before that feeling changed for both of us.

From her, and from Somel, who talked very freely with me, [5] I learned at last something of the viewpoint of Herland toward its visitors.

Here they were, isolated, happy, contented, when the booming buzz of our biplane tore the air above them.

Everybody heard it — saw it — for miles and miles, word [10] flashed all over the country, and a council was held in every town and village.

And this was their rapid determination:

"From another country. Probably men. Evidently highly civilized. Doubtless possessed of much valuable knowledge. [15] May be dangerous. Catch them if possible; tame and train them if necessary. This may be a chance to re-establish a bi-sexual state for our people."

They were not afraid of us — three million highly intelligent women — or two million, counting only grown-ups [20] — were not likely to be afraid of three young men. We thought of them as "Women," and therefore timid; but it was two thousand years since they had had anything to be afraid of, and certainly more than one thousand since they had outgrown the feeling.

[25] We thought — at least Terry did — that we could have our pick of them. They thought — very cautiously and farsightedly — of picking us, if it seemed wise.

All that time we were in training they studied us, analyzed us, prepared reports about us, and this information

---

[8] **biplane**：複葉機

[21] **it was two thousand years...**：この国が女性だけの国になった時期を指す。当時、戦争、火山爆発、奴隷の反乱がつづき、国の男たち全員と一部の女性が命を落とした。奴隷たちは若い女性と少女たちを支配しようともくろんでいたが、逆に、怒り狂った女たちに殺された。

was widely disseminated all about the land.

Not a girl in that country had not been learning for months as much as could be gathered about our country, our culture, our personal characters. No wonder their questions were hard to answer. But I am sorry to say, when we were at last brought out and — exhibited (I hate to call it that, but that's what it was), there was no rush of takers. Here was poor old Terry fondly imagining that at last he was free to stray in "a rosebud garden of girls" — and behold! the rosebuds were all with keen appraising eye, studying us.

They were interested, profoundly interested, but it was not the kind of interest we were looking for.

To get an idea of their attitude you have to hold in mind their extremely high sense of solidarity. They were not each choosing a lover; they hadn't the faintest idea of love — sex-love, that is. These girls — to each of whom motherhood was a lodestar, and that motherhood exalted above a mere personal function, looked forward to as the highest social service, as the sacrament of a lifetime — were now confronted with an opportunity to make the great step of changing their whole status, of reverting to their earlier bi-sexual order of nature.

Beside this underlying consideration there was the limitless interest and curiosity in our civilization, purely impersonal, and held by an order of mind beside which we were like — schoolboys.

It was small wonder that our lectures were not a success; and none at all that our, or at least Terry's, advances were so ill received. The reason for my own comparative success was at first far from pleasing to my pride.

"We like you the best," Somel told me, "because you seem

---

[1] **disseminate**：to spread widely
[17] **lodestar**：a guiding principle, an object of pursuit
[19] **sacrament**：神聖なもの

more like us."

"More like a lot of women!" I thought to myself disgustedly, and then remembered how little like "women," in our derogatory sense, they were. She was smiling at me, [5] reading my thought.

"We can quite see that we do not seem like — women — to you. Of course, in a bi-sexual race the distinctive feature of each sex must be intensified. But surely there are characteristics enough which belong to People, aren't there? [10] That's what I mean about you being more like us — more like People. We feel at ease with you."

Jeff's difficulty was his exalted gallantry. He idealized women, and was always looking for a chance to "protect" or to "serve" them. These needed neither protection nor service. [15] They were living in peace and power and plenty; we were their guests, their prisoners, absolutely dependent.

Of course we could promise whatsoever we might of advantages, if they would come to our country; but the more we knew theirs, the less we boasted.

[20] Terry's jewels and trinkets they prized as curios; handed them about, asking questions as to workmanship, not in the least as to value; and discussed not ownership, but which museum to put them in.

When a man has nothing to give a woman, is dependent [25] wholly on his personal attraction, his courtship is under limitations.

---

[4] **derogatory**：insulting

[12] **gallantry**：courteous attention to women, devotion to women

[20] **Terry's jewels and trinkets**：テリーは女性の気を引こうとして、宝石や小さな装身具をアメリカから持ってきたのだ。

[20] **curio**：a rare or unusual object

"Expelled"

Three of us were to go: Terry, because he must; I, because two were safer for our flyer, and the long boat trip to the coast; Ellador, because she would not let me go without her.

If Jeff had elected to return, Celis would have gone too — they were the most absorbed of lovers; but Jeff had no desire that way.

"Why should I want to go back to all our noise and dirt, our vice and crime, our disease and degeneracy?" he demanded of me privately. We never spoke like that before the women. "I wouldn't take Celis there for anything on earth!" he protested. "She'd die! She'd die of horror and shame to see our slums and hospitals. How can you risk it with Ellador? You'd better break it to her gently before she really makes up her mind."

Jeff was right. I ought to have told her more fully than I did, of all the things we had to be ashamed of. But it is very hard to bridge the gulf of as deep a difference as existed between our life and theirs. I tried to.

"Look here, my dear," I said to her. "If you are really going to my country with me, you've got to be prepared for a good many shocks. It's not as beautiful as this — the cities, I mean, the civilized parts — of course the wild country is."

"I shall enjoy it all," she said, her eyes starry with hope. "I understand it's not like ours. I can see how monotonous our quiet life must seem to you, how much more stirring yours must be. It must be like the biological change you told me about when the second sex was introduced — a far greater movement, constant change, with new possibilities of growth."

I had told her of the later biological theories of sex, and

---

[2] **Terry, because he must**：ある夜、テリーは妻アリマの寝室に潜んで待ち伏せし、彼女を力づくで襲おうとしたが、アリマほか数名に取り押さえられ、やがて国外退去を命じられた。

[9] **degeneracy**：堕落

she was deeply convinced of the superior advantages of having two, the superiority of a world with men in it.

[5] "We have done what we could alone; perhaps we have some things better in a quiet way, but you have the whole world — all the people of the different nations — all the long rich history behind you — all the wonderful new knowledge. Oh, I just can't wait to see it!"

編注者紹介

前沢浩子　獨協大学外国語学部教授　1961年生まれ　津田塾大学大学院博士課程満期退学　専門はイギリス演劇

畔柳和代　東京医科歯科大学教養部教授　1967年生まれ　東京大学大学院博士課程満期退学　専門は現代アメリカ文学

吉田朋正　首都大学東京人文科学研究科准教授　1968年生まれ　東京都立大学大学院博士課程満期退学　専門は現代アメリカ文学

Martin Nuttall　元東京医科歯科大学教養部外国人教師(2001年3月まで)　1960年生まれ　ケンブリッジ大学卒　エセックス大学大学院修了　専門は応用言語学

KENKYUSHA
〈検印省略〉

PRISM（プリズム）

2001年10月31日　初版発行　　2023年11月30日　15刷発行

編注者　前沢浩子・畔柳和代・吉田朋正・Martin Nuttall
発行者　吉田尚志
発行所　株式会社　研究社
　　　　〒102-8152　東京都千代田区富士見2-11-3
　　　　電話　03-3288-7711（編集）
　　　　　　　03-3288-7777（営業）
　　　　振替　00150-9-26710
印刷所　図書印刷株式会社

整版・レイアウト：㈲十歩　装丁：金野伸久（十歩）
ISBN 978-4-327-42158-8　C1082　Printed in Japan

SCOPE

前沢浩子　畔柳和代　吉田朋正　Martin Nuttall
編注

Earth, Life, language, Timeの4つのテーマを柱に、文系・理系を問わず広く大学生一般が興味を示すと思われるテキストを12本収録。TOEFLなど各種試験のリーディング対策にも十分対応。姉妹版PRISMと併せて使うことで、効果満点!!

SCOPEの内容

Earth
A New Shade of Green　To save the planet, we must embrace technology as well as trees (1988)　by Walter Truett Anderson
Our Stolen Future (1996)　by Theo Colborn, Dianne Dumanoski and John Peterson Myers
Walden (1854)　by Henry David Thoreau

Life
Gulliver's Travels (1726)　by Jonathan Swift
Longevity and the Barren Aristocrat (1998)　by Daniel E. L. Promislow
The Selfish Gene (1976)　by Richard Dawkins

Language
My Fair Lady (1956)　by Alan Jay Lerner
But Is It Language? (1997)　by Roger Fouts and Stephen Tukel Mills
Say What You Mean　Misunderstanding Between the Sexes (1999)　by Martin Nuttall

Time
The Arrow of Time (1988)　by Stephen Hawking
Ellipsis (1993)　by Alain de Botton
Speak, Memory (1966)　by Vladimir Nabokov